STEPHEN AND HALEY HARRISON

DISCIPLE THEM

A DISCIPLESHIP WORKBOOK
TO HELP OUR KIDS WALK WITH JESUS

Disciple Them: A Discipleship Workbook To Help Our Kids Walk With Jesus

ISBN 9798339128663   Copyright © 2024 by Stephen and Haley Harrison.

All rights reserved.

All Scripture quotations, unless otherwise indicated, are taken from the Holy Bible, New International Version®, NIV®. Copyright ©1973, 1978, 1984, 2011 by Biblica, Inc.™ Used by permission of Zondervan. All rights reserved worldwide. www.zondervan.com. The "NIV" and "New International Version" are trademarks registered in the United States Patent and Trademark Office by Biblica, Inc.™

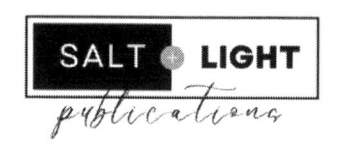

SALT LIGHT
publications

Dedicated to our three wonderful children Kylee, Abby, and Tate.

You are God's gift to us. We are proud of you and love you dearly.

Thank you for loving Jesus and walking with Him.

"I have no greater joy than to hear that my children are walking in the truth."

-3 John 4

CONTENTS

1. Love God
2. Love People
3. Love Jesus
4. Love the Word
5. Love the Holy Spirit
6. Love to Pray
7. Love the Least
8. Love the Church
9. Love Your Friends
10. Love Your Spouse
11. Love Your Kids
12. Be Life-Giving
13. Be in God's Will
14. Be On Mission
15. Be Quick to Listen
16. Be Slow to Speak
17. Be Slow to Anger
18. Be a Doer of the Word
19. Be in Community
20. Be a Hard Worker
21. Be a Servant
22. Be Physically Fit
23. Be Thankful
24. Be Loving
25. Be Joyful
26. Be Peaceful
27. Be Patient
28. Be Kind
29. Be Good
30. Be Faithful
31. Be Gentle
32. Be Self-Controlled
33. Be Humble
34. Be Gracious
35. Be Forgiving
36. Be Generous
37. Be Compassionate
38. Be a Good Neighbor
39. Be and Make Disciples
40. Be a Witness
41. Be Sexually Pure
42. Be Content
43. Spiritual Warfare
44. Repentance
45. Your Identity in Christ
46. Conflict Resolution
47. Biblical Manhood
48. Biblical Womanhood
49. How to Say Yes and No
50. Listen to the Holy Spirit
51. God's Faithfulness
52. God's Character
53. God's Love
54. Avoid Sin
55. Avoid Foolishness
56. Avoid Laziness
57. Avoid Pride
58. Avoid Gossip
59. Avoid Selfishness
60. Guard Your Heart
61. Guard Your Mind
62. Guard Your Eyes
63. Guard Your Mouth
64. Guard Your Emotions

65. Guard Your Time
66. Guard Your Talents
67. Fear
68. Loneliness
69. Disappointment
70. Grief
71. Uncertainty
72. Hurt
73. Wisdom
74. Having a Bad Day
75. Money
76. Purpose
77. Freedom
78. Where's God?
79. Taking a Stand
80. Don't Give Up

"I write to you, dear children, because you know the Father..."

-1 John 2:14a

HEY KIDS!

While listening to a sermon on 1 John 2, we heard the pastor read verse 14, "I write to you, dear children, because you know the Father". We sensed the Holy Spirit's prompting us to write some truths and wisdom based on God's Word – to you! I asked your mom if she would write it with me. She said yes! We wrote it from past conversations and times of discipleship at the dinner table, on car rides, and any moment when we discussed Jesus and his Word with you. We have taught and modeled most of these lessons to you in various ways at different moments in your lives. Our desire in writing this book is to give you more than practical information and advice. We desire you to possess biblical framework you can reference and reuse in your lives and in your own parenting one day. As parents, we want more for you than to have a good education and be good people. It's our greatest desire in life that you know and walk with the Father, Son, and Holy Spirit relationally. We want you to be fully devoted followers of Jesus in all areas of life. It can be challenging, but it is possible for every believer "to shine like stars" in a "crooked and perverse generation" (Philippians 2:15). We must disciple you to "hold firmly to the Word of life" (2:16). We pray you would teach these to your kids one day in your own way and the discipleship cycle would continue for many generations until the Lord's return.

We also want this to be a book other parents can use to teach their children to "love the Lord with all their heart, soul, mind, and strength and love their neighbor as themselves" (Matthew 22:37-39). As Christian parents, we are entrusted by God to disciple our children in the Word, will, and ways of the Lord, whatever their ages and in all their stages. To sum up this book in one sentence, I'd say, "Children, keep loving, living, and looking to Jesus for everything!" There are many other topics beyond this book that should be discussed. Allow the Holy Spirit and his Word to guide your conversations over a lifetime of discipling your children in the Lord.

We thank God for you and love you more than you'll ever know!
Dad and Mom
September 2024

HEY PARENTS!

We wrote this book to help parents disciple their children in many different practical topics. Parents are the primary disciple maker of their children. For some parents, they will be able to start with lesson one and continue in order through the whole book. Some parents will need to use this resource as a reference tool, selecting the devotion that best helps them in the moment. Some parents will need to skip certain topics because their children are too young. Some parents will need to revisit lessons in loving faith. We encourage you to use these lessons as a guide as you disciple your children. Feel free to modify them and insert your own testimony or experience. Allow the Holy Spirit to bring other Scriptures to mind. We intend these lessons to be guides that can be adapted or used exactly as written – your choice. The point is that you are spending time with your children in the Scriptures, prayer, and discussion about God. That's discipleship!

We also encourage to you to build lessons like these into your daily routine with your children. Whether it's at mealtime, bedtime, before school, or some other time, the anticipation you build as you develop this habit of spending time in the Lord with them is priceless. We developed these lessons and discipled our kids over meals, conversations in the car, and several other daily practices. Do the same! The goal is to use this resource (one of many out there) as a tool to build you and your children's faith in Christ.

Remember the discipleship challenge God gives parents in Deuteronomy 6:4-9:

> Hear, O Israel: The Lord our God, the Lord is one. Love the Lord your God with all your heart and with all your soul and with all your strength. These commandments that I give you today are to be on your hearts. Impress them on your children. Talk about them when you sit at home and when you walk along the road, when you lie down and when you get up. Tie them as symbols on your hands and bind them on your foreheads. Write them on the doorframes of your houses and on your gates.

Take time to pray before, during, and after each lesson. Never discount the power of praying parents! We've seen God work in our kid's lives in miraculous ways. At times, we weren't sure they comprehended the spiritual significance in our discipleship efforts, but we've been reminded time and time again it's the Spirit that changes hearts and leads all of us into His truth. The Holy Spirit and His Word bring correction and give instruction. They guide and help us. God wants us to grow in a relationship with him. Scripture is more than "quit doing that" or "fix what's broken". It's God's love letter that points us to Jesus. We desire your kids to grow more in love with a perfect Savior. These lessons can help their spiritual journey, but its bigger than behavior modification. We want them to help your children to know and follow Jesus. Remember, whatever time you spend talking to your kids about Jesus will not be wasted. His Word accomplishes all God desires (Isaiah 55:11).

HOW TO USE THESE DISCIPLESHIP LESSONS

Each lesson has several key parts that are designed to be interactive. There is a **BIBLE VERSE** to point you to the truth of God's Word. Try to memorize, write it, read it out loud, refer to it often. The **SOMETHING TO THINK ABOUT** section is meant to be read out loud and help prompt more thoughts about the topic and Scripture. Feel free to add your own thoughts as the Spirit leads! The **TRUTH TO TREASURE** is the main take away point of the lesson. Say: "Here's the truth to treasure from today's lesson". This is what you want them to remember from the devotional. The **REFLECTION QUESTIONS** help review the lesson but call you to action. Use them or feel free to use your own questions. The point is to do what you've learned. The **NOTES** is just that – a notes section. Write down statements your child makes, the date you did the devotional, follow up ideas, and anything the Spirit prompts. Each **ACTION STEP** is just a way for you and your child to interact in a fun and memorable way to learn the biblical principle. Enjoy that time with your child! Each lesson ends with **OUR PRAYER FOR YOU**. This is a sample prayer to pray with your child as you ask God to help you grow closer to Him and be more like Him.

Trust God as he uses you to disciple your kids. We are praying for you!
Stephen and Haley Harrison

LOVE GOD

Bible Verse:

"Jesus replied: 'Love the Lord your God with all your heart and with all your soul and with all your mind.' This is the first and greatest commandment. And the second is like it: 'Love your neighbor as yourself.'"
— Matthew 22:37-39

Something to Think About:

The greatest thing you could ever do is have a relationship with God. He loves you with an everlasting love (Jeremiah 31:3) because He is love (1 John 4:8, 16)! He loved you so much that He sent His Son Jesus to die on the cross for your sins (John 3:16). I (Dad) gave my life to Christ when I was seven and have been growing closer to Him and more like Him every day since. I (Mom) made a decision for Christ when I was seven, but believe it was when I was in college that I was truly saved. Whatever you do, give your life to Jesus, and don't stop living for Him. **(Parents, share your salvation story at this time).**

One Scripture that has always shaped how we love God and love others is called the Great Commandment (Matthew 22:37-39). Jesus said these statements sum up and fulfill the Law and the Prophets. In other words, they are the most important commands He gives us.

Truth to Treasure:
God loves you and wants you to love Him and others!

This means you can't function in your Christian walk without them. We must fall more in love with Jesus and learn how He wants us to love others.

In short, we pray your whole lives are full of loving God and loving others. Don't ever separate these. One of the best ways to experience and grow in God's love is by spending time with Him. Just as you need to spend time with friends and family to grow in your love for them, you must also spend time with God. Invest time daily praying and reading the Word. The more time you spend with God, the more time you'll want to spend with Him!

Reflection:

1. How does knowing God loves you unconditionally (no matter what) grow your love for Him?

2. How does loving God and knowing his love help you love other people?

3. How is your relationship with God growing?

Notes:

THE HEART OF GOD *Action Step:*
Draw a heart on a large posterboard. Have your child write words inside the heart to describe God's love. Examples: loving, generous, caring, patient, powerful, plenty, calming. Draw a heart on the other side. Write words inside the heart to describe how they love God. Examples: obey, worship, pray, give, serve, follow, change. Discuss how we love God with our heart, soul, mind, and strength.

Our Prayer For You:

We pray our love for God increases more and more as you see how much He loves you! Jesus, show us how much you love us as we read Your Word and pray. May we extend your love to others so they will see your love for them as well. In Jesus' name, Amen.

LOVE PEOPLE

Bible Verse:

"Jesus replied: 'Love the Lord your God with all your heart and with all your soul and with all your mind.' This is the first and greatest commandment. And the second is like it: 'Love your neighbor as yourself.'"
— Matthew 22:37-39

Something to Think About:

One Bible verse we always prayed at night before bed with you was Matthew 22:37-39. It reminded us to love God and love people. We're sure you've noticed how others are sometimes "unlovable" (we're never that way, right?). What we are learning (and you probably are as well) is our love for others is often shallow or absent apart from knowing and experiencing God's love. It is out of being loved by God and loving Him in return that we can love others how He would love them.

A Scripture the indwelling Holy Spirit often reminds us of is Romans 5:8: *"But God demonstrates His own love for us in this: While we were still sinners, Christ died for us."* Every time we read or remember that verse, we're reminded that WHILE we were not worthy of love, WHILE we had not promised to love Him in return, WHILE we had not changed, and WHILE we had no hope of changing ourselves, Jesus loved us.

Truth to Treasure: **We know how to love others by the way God loves us!**

We've committed Matthew 22:37-39 to memory. It is usually one of the first Bible verses we think about each day. Why? We use it to pray, "God, help us fall more in love with you today and love people the way you do." These verses are what we call "refrigerator verses". They are life verses – words to live (and love) by! We guarantee if you center your life in these words of Christ, you'll never be disappointed. You'll be blessed and be a blessing! We pray we've loved you in this way.

Reflection:

1. How does God's love help us love others?

2. What are some of the qualities of God's love?

3. Who can you express God's love to today? How will you do that?

Notes:

ACT OF KINDNESS *Action Step:*

Loving others can be very simple and practical. Create a card that says "Act of Kindness" with a Bible verse like Proverbs 11:24, Luke 6:31, Ephesians 4:32a. Write on it something like: "We hope this act of kindness has displayed God's love for you. We are thankful for you and prayed for you." Think of ways to love others as you give them a card and serve them.

Our Prayer For You:

Lord, may we "grasp how wide, long, high, and deep is the love of Christ" (Ephesians 3:17). May we extend your love in hopes others will discover your great for love them. Help us "love in actions and in truth" (1 John 3:18). Thank you for loving us first (1 John 4:19). In Jesus' name, Amen.

LOVE JESUS

Bible Verse:

"Anyone who loves their father or mother more than me is not worthy of me; anyone who loves their son or daughter more than me is not worthy of me. Whoever does not take up their cross and follow me is not worthy of me."
-Matthew 10:37-38

Something To Think About:

What does it mean to love Jesus? We all know the song, "Jesus Loves Me", and He does! It was God's love expressed through the sacrificial gift of Jesus on the cross for our sins that displays His great affection for us (John 3:16; 1 John 4:7-12). Loving Jesus is done in response to knowing His great love for us.

We use the same word "love" in many ways to describe varying degrees of adoration for anything from tacos to family. I think saying, "I love tacos" and "I love my mom" and "I love Jesus" are vastly different. Although tacos are very yummy, it's almost as if we should reserve the word "love" for only the most important things.

In Matthew 10:37-38, Jesus told his disciples to love him more than we love our children, parents, and anything else (friends, material possessions, boyfriend, girlfriend, pets, etc.). He wasn't saying we should abandon our love for them. He was simply helping us remember to place him first in all our relationships and affections. Truthfully, we will love others in the purest sense of the word when our love for Jesus is the top priority.

Truth To Treasure:
If we love Jesus, we will treasure Him most!

How do we love Jesus? We spend time with him in his Word, learn about him, allow him to shape our desires, and seek to be and do what pleases him. Jesus said we must "take up our cross and follow him". This means we allow Jesus to show us what life is about by seeking him first and following him in all ways.

Reflection:

1. What do you think it means to love Jesus?

2. What does "taking up our cross" look like as we think about how Jesus went to the cross?

3. Jesus said, "If you love me, you will keep my commandments" (John 14:15). How do love and obedience work together?

Notes:

A JESUS PLAY *Action Step:*

Ask: "What is your favorite Jesus Bible story?" Find it in the Bible and read it out loud. Reenact the story using items to make costumes and props. Be creative! Involve others! After you practice (dress rehearsal), put on a play for family and friends. Some good Bible stories to act out are: The Good Samaritan, The Prodigal Son, the healing of man lowered through roof, the Woman at the Well, etc.

Our Prayer For You:

Jesus, help us love you like you love us. Love is more than a feeling. Your love is foundational and transforms us. Because you loved us, we desire to love you above everything else. Help us walk with you, obey you, and please you. In Jesus' name, Amen.

LOVE THE WORD

Bible Verse:

"All Scripture is God-breathed and is useful for teaching, rebuking, correcting, and training in righteousness, so that the servant of God may be thoroughly equipped for every good work."

- 2 Timothy 3:16-17

Something to Think About:

We own a lot of Bibles. You probably do as well. We probably have at least one of each modern English translation – and even some in other languages. I (dad) have my parent's Bibles and even a couple family heirloom Bibles from my childhood. Owning Bibles is not the same thing as reading them. Reading them is not the same thing as loving the Word of God. We should read the Bibles we own and allow God to change our lives through his eternal Word. The reason we love the Bible is because we love Jesus. All the Old Testament points to Jesus the Messiah, all the gospels are about Jesus' ministry, and all the New Testament from Acts on point us back to Jesus. The Bible is more than another history or self-help book. It is the living, active, transforming, inspired and perfect message from God to us. It is how God reveals who He is and His plan for our lives.

Truth to Treasure:
God's Word is true and useful for everything in life.

Second Timothy 3:16-17 tells us Scripture is from God and is useful in a lot of ways. It doesn't just give us God's opinions, as if there are others that are more important. It provides righteous instruction so we can be equipped to know God and do his will in life. The Word is alive and changes our souls (Hebrews 4:12). This means God's Word informs how our personality, thoughts, feelings, words, actions, desires, and emotions should look. How do we love God's Word more? Read it every day. Meditate on what you read. Pray and ask the Holy Spirit how to apply it to your life. Memorize it so you can use it when you need it. Pray it. Use it in conversation. Go to it first for advice and wisdom. Allow it to point you to Jesus!

Reflection:

1. Why is loving God's Word important?

2. What's your favorite Bible verse?

3. How does the Bible equip us for every good work?

Notes:

A GOOD PLAN *Action Step:*
Help your child develop a Bible reading plan. There are several on the YouVersion Bible App for kids. Some of them will read to them (if they can't read just yet). Set a time each day to read the Bible with your child. Start at the beginning of a book and read a story or chapter each night. Take time to discuss what you are reading (even along the way). Get caught by your kids on purpose reading your Bible.

Our Prayer For You:

Thank you, Jesus, for your Word. Help us read, study, memorize, and apply it so we may see you clearer and follow you better. We invite you to teach, correct, train, and rebuke us any way you need to. We believe your Word is true and from you. Thank you for loving us enough to give us the Bible! In Jesus' name, Amen.

LOVE THE HOLY SPIRIT

Bible Verse:

"And I will ask the Father, and he will give you another Advocate to help you and be with you forever– the Spirit of truth. The world cannot accept him because it neither sees him nor knows him. But you know him, for he lives with you and will be in you."   - John 14:16-17

Something to Think About:

We used to think the Holy Spirit was weird. Truthfully, we didn't know much about him, and the KJV translation "Holy Ghost" made him seem even more mysterious. The church we grew up in didn't teach much about the Spirit. Thankfully, we had some people use the Scripture to disciple us in the person of the Holy Spirit. We also had some people misrepresent the Spirit in various ways. We learned the Spirit wasn't weird - people were at times! The Holy Spirit is the gift we receive at salvation, and He is our friend and helper who continually points us to Jesus.

You'll need help in life with a whole lot of things from a whole lot of people. Don't try to do this life without others. All of us need community. While you'll have many people in your life that will be great blessings, there are none greater than the one with the Spirit God gives us at salvation. God sent the third person of the Trinity, the Holy Spirit, to live in you and be with you. Jesus called the Holy Spirit our Helper, Comforter, and Advocate. The good news is he never stops filling us with more of himself (Ephesians 5:18).

Truth to Treasure:
The Holy Spirit lives in you and will always be with you!

The Holy Spirit empowers us to follow Jesus. He reminds us of everything Jesus taught (John 14:26), convicts us of sin (John 16:8), guides us to truth (John 16:13), and gives us His power to be witnesses for Jesus (Acts 1:8). He gives us wisdom (Ephesians 1:17) and helps when we are weak (Romans 8:26). We pray you grow in "the fellowship of the Holy Spirit" (2 Corinthians 13:14) as you walk with Jesus.

Reflection:

1. What is your first impression when you hear someone say "The Holy Spirit"?

2. How does the Holy Spirit help you in life?

3. What questions do you have about the Holy Spirit?

Notes:

A MIGHTY WIND *Action Step:*
Jesus compares the Holy Spirit to the mystery and power of the wind (John 3). Go outside if it's windy or turn on a fan. Say: "We can't see the wind, but we can feel it, see leaves blowing, paper moving, etc." We can't see the Spirit, but He's in us and we can respond to His filling. Just as the wind moves things, the Spirit moves us to love, serve, and obey. The Spirit wants to comfort, teach, guide, and help us.

Our Prayer For You:

Lord, thank you for the gift of your Holy Spirit when we are saved. Thank you for filling us more and more with your Spirit. We need your gifts, fruit, leading, help, correction, wisdom, and fellowship. Help us to understand and cooperate with your Spirit. Holy Spirit, thank you for living in us and leading us to Jesus! Amen.

LOVE TO PRAY

Bible Verse:

"Do not be anxious about anything, but in every situation, by prayer and petition, with thanksgiving, present your requests to God."
- Philippians 4:6

Something to Think About:

A gracious gift God gives us is the ability to connect with him anywhere, anytime, and about anything through prayer. Prayer is more than asking for help in a moment of crisis. You've probably heard someone say they've done everything but pray. I'm not sure of the original author, but I like the quote "Prayer isn't our last resort. It's our first option." While thankfully we can go to God in crisis, prayer is worship. It's something we should do multiple times a day every day – really all day long. It's how we communicate with God in response to His Word, align with His will, and walk in His ways. It's how we grow in relationship with Him.

Prayer is our lifeline with God. Perhaps that's why Paul said to "pray continuously" (1 Corinthians 5:17). Practically, we like to start our day off with prayer. I (dad) usually lay in the bed for about thirty minutes and pray each morning because I can be still and listen with almost no distractions. I (mom) have a quiet time of prayer and reading Scripture in my favorite chair after everyone is off to work and school each day. I (dad) pray a lot when I am driving. I have a long habit of praying for hospitals and churches when I pass them. I (mom) try to pray immediately when I discover someone's need. We both have found it best when someone asks for prayer to say, "Let's pray now" so we don't forget.

Truth To Treasure:

Prayer is our lifeline with God.

A guide we've often used to pray is A.C.T.S. – Adoration, Confession, Thanksgiving, and Supplication. This helps us express love, repentance, gratitude, and needs to God who loves us and is always listening. We love to pray!

Reflection:

1. What is your favorite time and place to pray?

2. Do you ever get "stuck" in your prayer life? How do you remedy that?

3. What questions do you have about prayer?

Notes:

PRAYER CLOSET Action Step:
Find a good closet in your home with an open wall you can turn into a prayer wall. Gather missionary cards from your church, note cards you can write on, and other ways to make prayer lists. Place a picture of your family and others that need prayer on the wall. Grab a cushion/pillow, notebook, Bible, and other items to make it more comfortable and inviting. Encourage your child to pray there every day.

Our Prayer For You:

Jesus, thank you that we can always pray to you and for hearing and answering us. Thank you for praying for us! Help us grow in continual conversation with you and weave prayer into the fabric of our daily lives. Help us to listen and be still. Help us trust you more as we pray. Teach us to pray. In Jesus' name, Amen.

LOVE THE LEAST

Bible Verse:

"The King will reply, 'Truly I tell you, whatever you did for one of the least of these brothers and sisters of mine, you did for me.'"
— Matthew 25:40

Something to Think About:

When we serve "the least of these", we are serving Jesus himself. Those are Jesus' words, not ours. What are "the least of these"? In Matthew 25:34-40, Jesus lists several people who he says we must serve as his church. Jesus lists those in need of food, water, clothing, healing, fellowship, and freedom. These are those whom the world tends to overlook - the poor, abused, and forgotten. Jesus tells us when we do (or don't) serve these, we do (or don't) serve him. That's powerful – serving others is worshiping Jesus!

We've tried to model serving Jesus by serving others over the years. We've worked in food pantries together. We've sponsored and written words of hope about Jesus to kids around the world. You've seen us serve in prison, foster, and pregnancy center ministries. We've served in homeless shelters, orphanages, nursing homes and bought food, gas, and shelter for many strangers who the Lord has allowed to cross our paths. There are so many opportunities to serve those in Matthew 25. Don't miss them!

Truth to Treasure:

When we love the least of these, we love Jesus.

When Jesus says "the least", he doesn't mean unimportant. Out of his list in Matthew 25, he doesn't tell us who is the least of these. Whomever the world calls "the least" or most insignificant, that's whom we must serve in Jesus' name. We must care, provide, serve, and love people like Jesus would. We must serve them as we would serve Jesus. He calls them his brothers and sisters and they are ours as well. Keep loving people. Keep loving Jesus.

Reflection:

1. Who does Jesus tell us to serve in Matthew 25? Can you list examples of these today?

2. Why does Jesus equate serving others with serving himself?

3. How can you serve "the least of these" this week?

Notes:

Action Step:

FOSTERING LOVE
Talk about who you know that fosters or has adopted. You may need to describe what these are. How can you serve these families practically this week? Examples: cook a meal, include those kids in your family activities, etc. Maybe you have a foster care ministry in your area. How can you serve them? Donate clothing or supplies? Organize? Clean?

Our Prayer For You:

Jesus, thank you for loving us. There are many times we are unlovable and unable to return your love. Thank you for showing us "the least of these" is not someone else – it is you! It's how you loved us. It's how we want to love others. Help us to love in action and truth. In Jesus' name, Amen.

LOVE THE CHURCH

Bible Verse:

"If I am delayed, you will know how people ought to conduct themselves in God's household, which is the church of the living God, the pillar and foundation of the truth." -1 Timothy 3:15

Something to Think About:

What's your first memory of church? What's your last? We pray they are good and life-giving. We remember the first day we took you to church after each of you were born. People flooded us, wanting to get a good look at you. We were so proud - and still are! We took you to a building, but the people that surrounded us that day were the church. Every born-again follower of Jesus is a member of his church. Those, and many others over the years, are the ones that have loved, served, and grown closer to Jesus with us.

Paul called the church "God's household" in 1 Timothy 3:15. That means family. We are God's family – He is our Father, and we are his adopted sons and daughters. As "the church of the living God", we are a community of faith who gather to worship Jesus and uphold "the pillar and foundation of the truth". Church is not something we attend once a week. It is who we are daily. What draws us together on Sunday and on various other times and spaces? Jesus!

Truth to Treasure:
The Church is the household of the living God.

Matthew 16:18 tells us Jesus will build his church and the gates of Hades will not overcome it. The church belongs to Jesus. While we gather, serve, and worship, he alone builds it. Many organizations are worth our involvement, but none are more alive and eternal than the church. Whatever you do, be faithful to a local body of believers. Don't let gossip, hurt, or anything keep you from being the church of the living God. Jesus is worth it. So is his church.

Reflection:

1. What is your best definition of church?

2. Why is it important to attend, serve, and worship in a local church?

3. What makes church great? What causes it to suffer?

Notes:

SERVE AT CHURCH *Action Step:*
Describe how there are many ways to serve at your local church. Make a list of those ways. Ask: "Where are we serving at church? How does our church need us to serve? What can we do this week to serve at our church?" Perhaps it is pulling weeds or planting flowers. Maybe you could serve by cleaning a room or making copies for a class. Find a practical way to serve your church this week.

Our Prayer For You:

Jesus, thank you for saving us and making us part of your church. We love you and your bride. You call the church a body and every part of it is important. Help us to stay on the mission you gave us as the church – to glorify you, share your gospel, and make disciples. In Jesus' name, Amen.

LOVE YOUR FRIENDS

Bible Verse:

"There is no greater love than to lay down one's life for one's friends. You are my friends if you do what I command you…I have called you friends…"
– John 15:13-15

Something to Think About:

Scripture says, "A friend loves at all times" (Prov. 17:17a). We've had some great friends over the years who have loved us well. I (dad) have a couple of close friends from high school. I (mom) have a best friend in my sister and a friend from high school. You have a lot of good friends. We think of friends like Jillian, Maggie, and Mason. Everybody wants and needs friends. The Bible tells us if we want friends, we must be friendly (Prov. 18:24a). There are many examples of true friendship in the Bible like David and Jonathan. David showed kindness to Jonathan (2 Sam. 9:7) and Jonathan was loyal to David (1 Sam.18:1-5). True friends stick with you in hard times. Ruth told Naomi, "Where you go I will go, and where you stay I will stay. Your people will be my people and your God my God" (Ruth 1:16).

Truth to Treasure:
Good friends help us live and love like Jesus.

I'm thankful Jesus calls us friends (John 15:15). The Bible says God spoke to Moses "As one who speaks to a friend" (Exodus 33:11). One of the best qualities of a friend is someone who helps you to get closer to Jesus. Isn't that what the paralyzed man's four friends did (Mark 2:1-12)? Friends spend time together. Jesus, Lazarus, Mary, and Martha did this (Luke 10:38). Friends encourage (1 Thess. 5:11). Friends sacrifice (John 15:13). We must learn to choose our friends carefully (Prov. 12:26) as "bad company corrupts good morals" (1 Cor. 15:33). A sweet friend refreshes the soul and brings joy (Prov. 27:9). Gossip divides (Prov. 16:28). Unforgiveness destroys (Prov. 17:9). Pray for your friends. Be there for them in tough times (Prov. 17:17b). Remember, it's hard to make new old friends. Be the kind of friend you want.

Reflection:

1. What are the qualities of a good friend?

2. What harms friendships?

3. How is Jesus our best friend?

Notes:

Action Step:

A FRIEND LIST
Make a list of your and your child's friends. On a separate piece of paper, number these items: call, text, letter, meal, gift, time, pray, help. Discuss how these make friendships grow strong. Pray and think about which number should go beside each friend's name (multiple numbers are OK). Now decide when and how you will do these for your friends this next week.

Our Prayer For You:

Jesus, thank you for calling us friends. You are a friend that sticks closer than a brother. Help us be the kind of friend you are to us. Help us pursue friendships that bring us closer to you. Help us be the kind of friends we want to have. In Jesus' name, Amen.

LOVE YOUR SPOUSE

Bible Verse:

"Wives, submit yourselves to your own husbands as you do to the Lord…Husbands, love your wives, just as Christ loved the church and gave himself up for her." — *Ephesians 5:22a, 25a*

Something to Think About:

Marriage is a gift and a blessing from God. God created it in the beginning to be one man and one woman for a lifetime (Genesis 2:24). In the next chapter, sin entered the world and marriages have been struggling ever since. While there are no perfect marriages, God is perfect. He gives us the ability to love, serve, honor, and encourage one another. Only God can unite one man and one woman together as husband and wife. What he joins, we must not separate (Matthew 19:6).

We love being married to one another. You know our story well. We met at church as kids, dated as teenagers through college, and have been married almost 24 years as we write this book. We are each other's best friends. Paul said in Ephesians 5 that we must do our parts in marriage like he would. He defines and demonstrates love. He showed us how he submitted willingly to a loving Father. One of our favorite verses about marriage is found in 1 Peter 3 and describes how we should view marriage. Peter said we are "heirs together in this gracious gift of life" (v. 7). How we view God's gift of marriage and purpose for our lives will determine how we treat our spouses. In that same verse, Peter said the husband should honor, respect, and be considerate with our spouses.

Truth to Treasure:

Marriage is a gift and a blessing from God.

We have prayed for your future spouses since you were born. We have prayed God would gift to you believers who love and are growing in Jesus. If it is God's will for you to marry, we pray you find spouses as great as we did.

Reflection:

1. What do you think makes a good husband and wife?

2. Why do you think marriages sometimes struggle?

3. If it is God's will for you to marry, how can you prepare for that now?

Notes:

Action Step:

WEDDING PHOTO
Find several wedding photos (yours or general ones) and describe what happens at a wedding. What words are spoken? What do actions like exchanging rings and lighting candles represent? Talk about what vows, unity, joy, commitment, and other words mean in marriage. Pray with your child about the possibility of a future spouse. What should you pray for?

Our Prayer For You:

God, thank you for creating marriage and showing us in your Word how to be one as you and the Father are one. Help us understand your principles and learn to love and serve people, including our future spouses, as you would. Keep us from selfishness, envy, jealousy, and pride. Help us learn how to honor, respect, and be considerate with others. In Jesus' name, Amen.

LOVE YOUR KIDS

Bible Verse:

"Children are a blessing from the Lord, offspring a reward from him. Like arrows in the hands of a warrior are children born in one's youth. Blessed is the man whose quiver is full of them." – Psalm 127:3-5

Something to Think About:

Children are a blessing from the Lord! Yes, you have tremendously blessed us and we are very thankful God has entrusted us to be your parents! We are proud of you and love you! Loving kids, we have learned, is not giving them whatever they want but pointing them to Jesus. Psalm 127 says children are like arrows in a warrior's hands. Warriors used to make their own arrows. They would shape them in a way to ensure they flew straight and hit their intended target. The bow (structure) they placed them in and launched them from was equally as important. God has given you to us to shape you into the image of Christ and point you towards Him.

We are overjoyed that you love and follow Jesus. Each of you have grown in the Lord in many ways. God has used a lot of "structures" to do that (student ministry, church camp, D-Groups, etc.) but none are more important than the home. One day, if the Lord wills, you will have children. Don't let everyone else take the lead in shaping their impressionable lives. You do it! From an early age, show them how to love and live for Jesus. From reading the Bible with you to living it out in front of you, our goal has been to worship and please God with the gifts of kids he has entrusted to us.

Truth to Treasure:

Children are a blessing from the Lord.

The Apostle John said, "I have no greater joy than to hear my children walk in truth" (3 John 4). Parenting can be challenging at times – but completely worth it. You're worth it. We love being your parents. May God give you kids one day that have been as much a blessing to us that you have.

Reflection:

1. What do you think about being a parent one day?

2. What are good qualities of parents? What about good qualities of children?

3. How do you think parents and children succeed? What causes them to struggle?

Notes:

CUT CORNERS — Action Step:

This game illustrates how God's love grows every time we show it. Take a piece of paper and write a loving action in each corner. Ask: "How many corners are there?" (4). Cut one corner and give it to your child. Ask: "Now, how many corners are there?" (5). Write down two new ways to express love. Cut another corner. Now there are 6! Every time you give God's love away, it grows!

Our Prayer For You:

Jesus, thank you for the gift of children. We are thankful you give us the right to be called children of God (John 1:12). You are a good Father. We desire to be sons and daughters that please you. Help us model Jesus to our children and family. May our homes be a place where you are most important. In Jesus' name, Amen.

BE LIFE-GIVING

Bible Verse:

"The soothing tongue is a tree of life, but a perverse tongue crushes the spirit."
-Proverbs 15:4

Something to Think About:

One of the best ways to live on purpose for Jesus is to be life-giving. How do you do this? Only Jesus can give us new life. He gives spiritual life to our mortal bodies through His Spirit who is inside us. Romans 8:9 says, *"However, you are not in the flesh but in the Spirit, if indeed the Spirit of God dwells in you. But if anyone does not have the Spirit of Christ, he does not belong to Him."* Because we are born again and have the Spirit of God living in us, we are to be life-giving in all our ways. The way we talk and act should reflect that the Spirit of God lives in us.

One way to be life-giving is to stay in God's Word. As you read and apply it, you can use it in your everyday conversation. The Bible tells us be encouraging, peaceful, kind, patient, generous, and a host of other characteristics that only come from Jesus. The opposite of life-giving is life-taking. When we get "in the flesh", we revert to acting, talking, and thinking in a way opposite of our life in Christ.

Truth to Treasure:

Being life-giving is really walking in the Spirit.

Gossip, hate, and selfishness, and not life-giving. Praying for others is a good way to also be life-giving. Proactive prayers are when you ask, "How can I pray for you?".

Being life-giving is really walking in the Spirit (Galatians 5:25). We must allow the Spirit to lead us (Romans 8:14) into wisdom, truth, and righteousness. This will cause us to bear fruit from the Spirit (Galatians 5:22-23). There is no better way to be life-giving than to share the gospel – the good news of eternal life. In all you say and do, be Christlike. That's life-giving!

Reflection:

1. How do we become (and become more) life-giving?

2. Can you name some life-giving qualities of Jesus?

3. What are some characteristics that are not life-giving and opposite of Jesus?

Notes:

Action Step:

LIFE GIVING

Jesus gives us new life. Buy a couple of apples. Show a seed and say, "Life begins for an apple by planting this seed". Discuss how a seed, tree, and apples grow. Talk about how fruit is enjoyed because new life is formed. Enjoy eating an apple together. Discuss how rotten apples are not life giving or why trees sometimes die to show the opposite of life giving.

Our Prayer For You:

Jesus, thank you for giving us new life. We cannot be life-giving without your Holy Spirit living in us. Thank you for showing us how to act, talk, and think in a way that best represents you to others and most glorifies God. Help us to walk in your Spirit and share Jesus with others. In Jesus' name, Amen.

BE IN GOD'S WILL

Bible Verse:

"Therefore, do not be foolish, but understand what the Lord's will is."

-Ephesians 5:17

Something to Think About:

What's God's will for my life? That's a question we've asked several times and you probably have as well. Most people ask this question at important transitions in life like marriage, career, education, and even homeowning. Some people constantly live in confusion believing God's will is forever evasive. We think knowing and living in God's will is easier to understand than its sometimes made out to be.

God does have a will or plan for your life. He is not just concerned with the "big decisions of life", but also the everyday details as well. James 4:15 tells us, "If the Lord wills, we will do this or that." However, this should not paralyze you in decision making. We believe God's Word reveals how we are to live in the present. We shouldn't be more concerned with the mysteries of our future than the realities of our present. God's not trying to hide His will from you. While the Bible has specific things to do and not do, it is a book of principles.

Truth to Treasure: **The Holy Spirit teaches and leads us into God's will.**

We are to focus on living out what we know God wants us to do and trust he will reveal future steps as we do.

Good verses we choose to live by are Romans 12:1-2. We desire God to transform us instead of conforming to the world. It is God's will that we be sanctified or growing in holiness and Christlikeness (1 Thessalonians 4:3). He will equip us to do his will (Hebrews 13:21). His Spirit teaches and leads us to do his will (Psalm 143:10). You're never more in God's will than when you are worshipping him and making him known to others.

Reflection:

1. What do you think God's will is for everyone that is saved?

2. In what specific ways, places, and relationships can you live out God's will?

3. Is there an area of your life you are concerned is not in God's will?

Notes:

Action Step:

WHAT PLEASES GOD?
Being in God's will is doing what pleases Him. Write the words "kindness, gentleness, patience, compassion, forgiveness, love" on separate index cards. Have your child draw them one at a time out of a box. Have them give examples of how they can please God with each word. Ask: "What are some words/actions that do not please God?"

Our Prayer For You:

Jesus, thank you for helping us know your will for our lives. You desire us to worship and become more like you in every way. Your will for our lives matches the Father's. Holy Spirit teach and lead us into your will. Help me be committed to reading your Word and discovering more of your will in it. In Jesus' name, Amen.

BE ON MISSION

Bible Verse:

"One thing I ask from the Lord, this only do I seek: that I may dwell in the house of the Lord all the days of my life, to gaze on the beauty of the Lord and to seek him in his temple."   -Psalm 27:4

Something to Think About:

Have you ever wondered what God's mission for your life is? You know, your God given purpose. I (dad) remember wondering that when I was a teenager, especially as I approached graduation from high school. Although I had thoughts of being a pastor, I really wasn't sure what I was going to do for a living. The good news is God's mission for our lives can be discovered and lived out at any point in life and accomplished through any vocation. The work we do isn't our mission – it's one of the "vehicles" we use to carry it out.

David had it right in Psalm 27:4. His "one thing" he asked was to dwell with the Lord, gaze on his beauty, and seek him. David reminds us that the main mission of our lives, our purpose, is to worship the Lord. We can do that whatever job we have. We can do that single or married. We can do that with or without kids. Worshipping God can be done in "perfect" or not so perfect circumstances. Living out God's mission happens as we love the Lord with all our heart, soul, mind, and strength in every area of our lives.

Truth to Treasure: **The main mission of our lives is to worship the Lord.**

What keeps us from living on mission? The biggest hinderance to worshipping God with our lives is sin. Sin separates us from God. Repentance is the way to get back on God's mission. We worship God when we obey His Word, use our spiritual gifts, share the gospel, and make disciples. Growing closer to the Lord is God's mission for your life. You'll be most fulfilled in life when you make worshipping him the most important goal of life.

Reflection:

1. What is God's purpose for your life?

2. How can you live out God's purpose in the various areas of your life?

3. What keeps us from living on mission for God?

Notes:

Action Step:

RECORDING SCRIPTURE

One way we can live on mission is to share Jesus with others. In this activity, have your child record a Bible verse about the gospel on your phone. Then, send it to someone you know with a text of encouragement by letting them know God loves them and you are thinking and praying for them. Example Scriptures: John 3:16, Romans 10:9-10, 1 John 1:9

Our Prayer For You:

Jesus, you have the perfect plan for our lives. You created us to worship you through every area of our lives. The one thing we ask, dwell on, and seek is you. May we worship you through our relationships, vocation, and everything else. In Jesus' name, Amen.

BE QUICK TO LISTEN

Bible Verse:

"My dear brothers and sisters, take note of this: Everyone should be quick to listen, slow to speak and slow to become angry."

-James 1:19

Something to Think About:

You've heard us ask you many times, "Are you listening?" Someone once said speaking is telling what you know while listening is receiving what you don't know. Communication is two way – we speak and listen. James tells us we should listen more than we speak. Why is listening so important? Listening is an act of submission. It says to the one speaking what they have to say is important. This conveys respect, love, and care. Listening also conveys humility and teachability. It communicates you have much to learn and the desire to do so.

Listening to the Lord is important as he has much to say to us. When we read his Word, we should pause and listen for the Holy Spirit to lead us. When we listen to a preacher, we should take notes so we can seek to understand the message and apply it throughout the week. When we listen to a friend, we should look for ways to love and serve them.

Truth to Treasure:

Listening conveys respect, love, and care.

The Holy Spirit speaks to us through God's Word. Several times the Scripture says we should listen to what the Spirit is saying. When we hear others talk about God or the Word, we should ask ourselves does what they are saying glorify God, agree with God's Word, and accurately represent God's character. Sometimes we don't listen because we are distracted by so many things. Whatever you do, make sure you slow down and listen to those you love – especially the Lord. He has so much to say so don't miss His wisdom, counsel, and truth!

Reflection:

1. How can you become a better listener?

2. How does God "talk" to us?

3. What keeps us from hearing what God has to say to us?

Notes:

Action Step:
WHAT DID YOU SAY?
Prepare a word list with words spelled backwards. Practice saying those words. Say: I'm going to say a word that's spelled backwards. Listen carefully and tell me what the correct word is as it's spelled forward. Start easy and then harder. Examples: dog = God, yoj = joy, ecnad = dance Talk about how they had to listen before they spoke to be correct.

Our Prayer For You:

Jesus, thank you for speaking to us through your Word and Spirit. Help us to hear your truth and wisdom. We need your counsel and insight on everything. Keep me teachable and humble so I can receive your Word. Help me practice listening to those I love and learn how I can better love them. In Jesus' name, Amen.

BE SLOW TO SPEAK

Bible Verse:

"My dear brothers and sisters, take note of this: Everyone should be quick to listen, slow to speak and slow to become angry."

-James 1:19

Something to Think About:

Have you ever said something you regret? Perhaps you misspoke about a topic or even said something rude. James continues his practical advice after saying "be quick to listen" and says be "slow to speak". This doesn't mean we shouldn't talk but should choose our words carefully. This includes the timing and tone of our words as well. How and when we say something are just as important as what we say.

The Bible tells us we should speak with graciousness, wisdom, patience, honesty, and kindness. Proverbs 16:24 says, "Gracious words are like a honeycomb, sweetness to the soul and health to the body." Our words should not be divisive and abusive. Colossians 4:6 says, "Let your conversation be always full of grace, seasoned with salt, so that you may know how to answer everyone."

Truth to Treasure:

Our words should build, bless, and praise.

Jesus said our words are connected to our heart (Luke 6:45). Therefore, we must allow Jesus to change our heart so our words will be life-giving and edifying. When it comes to our words, we should use them to build, bless, and praise. We should build others up (Ephesians 4:29), bless people (Proverbs 11:25), and praise the Lord (Psalm 19:14). Our speech should be used for godly purposes. It's easy to get in the flesh with our words by gossiping, slandering, lying, and backbiting. No matter if it's in person, over text, or on social media, our words should be pleasing to the Lord. Everything we say should praise the Lord.

Reflection:

1. How important are the words we say to others?

2. How does God's Word affect our words?

3. Why is it hard to use our words to build, bless, and praise?

Notes:

Action Step:

NAME THAT SONG
Prepare a playlist of songs on your phone or device. Say: "I'm going to play a few seconds of a song, and I want you to guess it." Play 3 seconds, then 6 seconds, and so on until they guess it. See how many they can guess. Discuss the importance of listening before speaking and how it applies to this lesson.

Our Prayer For You:

Jesus, your Word is truth, wisdom, and insight for living. May our words match your Word as we build up and bless others. Help us to always praise you with our mouths. Please correct us before our words destroy relationships. Help us use words to ask for forgiveness when we've wronged others. In Jesus' name, Amen.

BE SLOW TO ANGER

Bible Verse:

"My dear brothers and sisters, take note of this: Everyone should be quick to listen, slow to speak and slow to become angry."

-James 1:19

Something to Think About:

Have you ever "blown your fuse"? One time our heater blew a fuse. The fuse wasn't the problem. We could have replaced it, but it would have blown again. The blown fuse let us know there was a bigger problem and kept our system from further damage. When we "blow a fuse" or become angry, it lets us know there's a deeper problem. James continues his practical advice by saying we should be "slow to become angry". His first two commands of being quick to listen and slow to speak help us from becoming angry. Our anger does not produce the kind of righteousness God desires (James 1:20).

People deal with anger differently. Some "stew" on it, never really conveying their inner anger. They just let their anger eat away at them, sometimes for years. Some "spew" it all over others in rants and destroy everyone in their path. The best way to deal with anger is allow God's Spirit and Word to correct our hearts. This sometimes means repenting, humbling oneself, and forgiving others. Anger can rob us from so many blessings from God and others.

Truth to Treasure:
Our anger does not produce the kind of righteousness God desires.

Paul said, "Be angry and do not sin" (Ephesians 4:26). There is such a thing as righteous anger. It is grief over sin when God or his Word is abused or injustice is done. The best thing to do in these situations is to pray, pause, and allow the Lord to check your motive before responding because, "A hot tempered person stirs up conflict, but the one who is patient calms a quarrel."

Reflection:

1. Look back at a time you were angry. How could you have responded differently?

2. How do we keep from reacting wrongly when we become angry?

3. How are "be quick to listen, slow to speak, and slow to anger" connected?

Notes:

Action Step:

THE ANGRY BALLOON

Ask what makes your child angry. Give other reasons for anger. For each response, blow a little air in the balloon. Discuss holding frustration, anger, resentment, feelings, words, etc. inside. What happens if we continue and let it out suddenly in anger? Explosion or fly around crazy. What's a safer way? Little, by little through prayer, forgiveness, humility, etc.

Our Prayer For You:

Jesus, thank you for helping us overcome anger. You were sometimes silent when accused and selective in your words when challenged. Thank you for giving us the ability to forgive others. Help me not to "stew" or "spew" in my anger. Help me be humble, gracious, repentant, and forgiving. In Jesus' name, Amen.

BE A DOER OF THE WORD

Bible Verse:

"Do not merely listen to the word, and so deceive yourselves. Do what it says."

-James 1:22

Something to Think About:

As we learned, James wants us to be quick to listen to God's Word (James 1:19). But James believes there's something more than only hearing it. We are to do what it says. We should listen, read, and study God's Word. It is meant to also be applied to our lives. James continues by saying if we listen to it but don't do what it says it's like looking in a mirror and forgetting what you look like (vv. 23-34). His point is the mirror would be pointless. Who looks at a mirror to see messed up hair only to do nothing about it? We know God's Word isn't pointless – it is perfect in every way. But, when we hear or read it and don't do what it says, it communicates to God we don't care about his perfect wisdom and truth.

James tells us to "look intently into the perfect law that gives freedom and continue in it" (v. 25). The Bible is not just a book of history we study for a test only to disregard its contents after taking a test. It's a book of liberty that helps us become

Truth to Treasure:
We need to know and do God's Word.

more like Jesus and please him in every way. It helps us know his will, follow his plan, and stay on mission. We need to know and do God's Word.

How do we "do what it says"? First, read it daily. As you read, pray. When we read God's Word, we pray something like "Holy Spirit, help me know and walk in your Word". As you read, ask the Holy Spirit if there is a command to obey, sin to confess or avoid, a promise to claim, or an example to follow. Memorizing Scripture can also be helpful when facing difficulties and decisions. Whatever you do, read and live out the Word of God.

Reflection:

1. Do you ever wonder how to apply the Scripture you have read?

2. How can prayer and Bible reading/study be helpful together?

3. What Scripture do you know that you need help living out?

Notes:

Action Step:
LIVE YOUR FAVORITE SCRIPTURE
Tell each other your favorite Bible verse. Ask: How can we live out this Bible verse? Talk about how you can practically live out that verse the next day. At the end of the day, discuss how you were a doer of the Word. Ask: How can we live that verse out better tomorrow? Pray God will give you opportunity to live out that verse in ways that honors him and others.

Our Prayer For You:
Jesus, thank you for giving us your Word to read and follow. As we read and study it, help us become more like you in every way. Help us put into practice your wisdom and truth. We desire to obey your Bible as it leads us into your presence and freedom. Help us live out your Word daily. In Jesus' name, Amen.

BE IN COMMUNITY

Bible Verse:

"So we cared for you. Because we loved you so much, we were delighted to share with you not only the gospel of God but our lives as well."
-1 Thessalonians 2:8

Something to Think About:

Have you ever felt alone? We all have at times. God's answer for loneliness and isolation is community. God built us for community. Another name for community is fellowship (*koinonia*). God designed us to belong in a family with brothers and sisters called the church. When we are saved, we are grafted into God's family. There no such thing as an "lone ranger" Christian. The church is Jesus' "body" (Colossians 1:24). God saved us to belong to the church and participate in all aspects of life together with other followers of Jesus Christ.

The body of Christ is lived out as the local church. This where we pray for one another, help, serve, love, and even share with one another. The local church is where we grow in our faith and participate in God's mission. One way this is accomplished is we serve with fellow believers in ministry. We can use our spiritual gifts with others in the church to serve people in practical ways.

Truth to Treasure:
God designed us to belong in a family called the local church.

Another way we grow in community is through small groups. This can be a serving team, a Sunday School class, a discipleship group, or any other form of a group within the local church. We grow better in smaller groups that pray, study the Word, and live out Scripture together.

The best way to grow in community in the local church is to show up and get involved. It may seem awkward to gather with new people in a new church, but they will quickly become forever friends in Christ. Don't sit back. Get involved in the community of God. We're so glad we have!

Reflection:

1. How important is it to be involved in the local church?

2. What are the benefits of community? How do we hurt when not in community?

3. In what ways are you involved in the community of your local church?

Notes:

Action Step:

COMMUNITY BUILDER
God designed us to be in community in the local church. Who do you not know at your church? Perhaps you see them on Sunday but do not know anything about them. How can you get to know them? What can you say to them next time you see them? Find a way to build community with someone at church this next week.

Our Prayer For You:

Thank you, Jesus, for teaching us community through your interaction with people in Scripture. We desire to be involved and engaged in the local church. Help us remember they are our brothers and sisters in the faith. Keep us faithful to those in the church in prayer, service, and spiritual growth. In Jesus' name, Amen.

BE A HARD WORKER

Bible Verse:

"Whatever you do, work at it with all your heart, as working for the Lord, not for human masters, since you know that you will receive an inheritance from the Lord as a reward. It is the Lord Christ you are serving."
–Colossians 3:23-24

Something to Think About:

Our parents taught the value of hard work. We learned to be faithful, dependable, and effective in our jobs. I (dad) have had a job since I was 13. I mowed lawns, worked in the garden, sold produce at the farmer's market, and worked in several retail stores before and during college. I (mom) worked for a few years outside the home and when we had our first child, I decided I wanted to stay home (which was also work). Work is more than a job. It's whatever you do. Paul told the Colossians to work at whatever they did with all their hearts as they would for the Lord. Whether that's our job, schoolwork, or community engagements, our work is worship.

Work is not a sin. God created it before the fall (Genesis 1:28). In the beginning, God placed Adam in charge of the garden of Eden. It was only after sin that work became labor intensive, strenuous, and done "by the sweat of your brow" (Genesis 3:17-24).

Truth to Treasure:

God designed us to work hard and rest well.

The Proverbs teach us the difference between laziness and hard work. One proverb tells us laziness is like a sluggard turning in his bed (26:14). Paul even said, "The one who will not work will not eat" (2 Thessalonians 3:10). God designed us to work. Working was one way man could spread God's glory throughout the world. As we carry out the work we have, we should seek to do so in the character of Christ. This is a great witness to those around us. We should work hard at whatever we do and avoid the temptation to be lazy. We should also learn to rest well in our work habits. This is pleasing to the Lord.

Reflection:

1. What does it look like to be a hard worker?

2. How does working hard please the Lord? How does foolishness not please him?

3. Is there an area of your life you don't like to work hard in? Why? How could you improve in that?

Notes:

Action Step:
HARD WORK REWARDS
God made us to work hard. Talk about the work each person in the family does (job, school, chores, etc.). How can you reward someone in your family for the hard work they do? Make them a card? Bake them a treat? Breakfast in bed? Do one of their chores? Be creative and show appreciation for hard work. Talk about how we can use our work as worship.

Our Prayer For You:

God, thank you for creating us to work hard. We desire to do so in a manner that is pleasing and worshipful to you. We understand our work is a way to model Christlikeness. Help us see you design in working and may others see you through our work. Help us see your purposes in the work we do. In Jesus' name, Amen.

BE A SERVANT

Bible Verse:

"For even the Son of Man did not come to be served, but to serve, and to give his life as a ransom for many."

—Mark 10:45

Something to Think About:

Jesus is the ultimate example of a servant. He gave his life on the cross for our sins. Jesus humbled himself by coming to earth, became fully man, yet fully God, and died for our forgiveness. In response to Jesus' gift of salvation, we should seek to serve him as we serve others. One of the best ways we can serve others is telling them about how Jesus saved us and desires to save them. This is sharing the gospel. Another way to serve people is by giving your resources to help those in need, sharing your time with those who need a helping hand or listening ear, and looking for needs in those around you.

There are many ways to serve people in your local Church. Find out how to serve in the ministries your church offers. This may be serving in the food pantry, children's ministry, music ministry, or as a greeter on Sunday morning. You can also serve in your neighborhood. Helping the elderly

Truth to Treasure:
Serving others displays Christ's love for them.

or a widow with a project or with yard work can be a great blessing. You can also serve in ministries that serve the homeless and disadvantaged. You can even serve people around the world. We serve orphanages in Haiti and the Philippines. You can also find out what some practical needs of your church's missionaries are and try to meet them.

Serving others is a great way to display Christ's love. Here's a pro tip: be a secret server – don't feel the need to tell anyone or post on social media. Just do it as worship to the Lord and help for those around you.

Reflection:

1. How is Jesus the greatest example of a servant?

2. How does serving others share Jesus' love for them?

3. What are some practical ways you can serve people around you?

Notes:

Action Step:

SERVING SWITCHAROO

How do you usually serve one another as a family? Does someone usually clean the kitchen, another usually take out the trash, etc.? Switch up chores. Do a couple of chores your mom usually does. Do a couple of chores your child usually does. Make one another's beds. This will hopefully give you a better appreciation for how you serve one another.

Our Prayer For You:

Jesus, thank you for serving us by humbling yourself and dying on the cross for our sins. Our service is worship to you in gratitude of your gift of salvation. As we serve others, may we not do it to be seen or earthly rewards. Help us serve with a Christ like heart and attitude in whatever way is needed. In Jesus' name, Amen.

BE PHYSICALLY FIT

Bible Verse:

"So I do not run aimlessly; I do not box as one beating the air. But I discipline my body and keep it under control, lest after preaching to others I myself should be disqualified."   -1 Corinthians 9:26-27

Something to Think About:

You may be asking yourself why this lesson is included in a spiritual devotional book. Well, God created our bodies, and they are the vehicle we use to display our personality and character as well as use our spiritual gifts and service to the Lord. The better care we take of our bodies, the better we can use them to glorify the Lord. There are sins of the flesh (body) we can commit that can harm our witness for Christ. Gluttony and laziness come to mind. Romans 12:1 tells us to present our bodies as living sacrifices for God that should be holy and pleasing to him.

Being physically fit includes exercise and diet. Eating healthy and maintaining a habit of working out are important for strength and stamina. They help our immune systems and even can promote emotional health. We are a triune being: spirit, soul, and body. You cannot disconnect those parts of you on this earth. They all affect the others. If we can prevent unnecessary health issues and even develop more energy for sharing Jesus and helping others grow in Christ, we should. Taking care of our bodies tells Jesus we are good stewards of the health and bodies he has given us.

Truth to Treasure: **We should strive to discipline our bodies as worship to Jesus.**

Paul said he disciplined his body. This includes saying no to sins of the flesh. Paul said his preaching would have been disqualified if his physical actions didn't align with the content of his ministry. Our bodies are temples of the Holy Spirit, so we should avoid anything that would be contrary to that including drugs and drunkenness. Grow spiritually and physically for Jesus.

Reflection:

1. How are physical and spiritual growth connected?

2. What are some ways you can grow in your physical health?

3. Can you think of any other Scriptures about being physically fit?

Notes:

Action Step:
EXERCISE CHALLENGE
Pick an exercise activity you can do together (run, walk, hike, pickleball, basketball, etc.). Plan a time you will do this together at least a couple times a week. Use this time to listen to praise songs. Ask: What's your favorite praise song? Why? See if you can discover any Bible references in the songs and look them up together (do an internet search if needed).

Our Prayer For You:

Jesus, we desire to grow spiritually and physically for your glory. Help me discipline my body in a way that strengthens my spiritual life and testimony. Help me form habits that promote physical growth as my body is a temple for your Spirit. Thank you for helping me grow in every area of life. In Jesus' name, Amen.

BE THANKFUL

Bible Verse:

"Rejoice always, pray continually, give thanks in all circumstances; for this is God's will for you in Christ Jesus."
-1 Corinthians 5:16-18

Something to Think About:

Our parents taught us to say thank you when others do something for you. We have also taught you to be thankful. Giving thanks can sometimes be hard because we are selfish. We should thank God every day in many ways through our prayer, devotion, and lifestyle. We should thank others with our words and actions as well. Returning someone's act of kindness with a similar action can be a blessing to both you and them.

One of the ways we stay thankful is found in 1 Corinthians 5:16-18. These are the shortest three verses you'll ever memorize. Two of the verses are only two words each. They are all connected. How do we rejoice always? We must pray continually and give thanks in all circumstances. How do we pray continually? We must be thankful and rejoice. You get the picture? When we do one, it helps us to do the others. When we forget to be thankful, it's most likely we haven't been praying and rejoicing in the Lord. When we spend time with Jesus, he reminds us about all we are to be thankful for.

Truth to Treasure: **Spending time with Jesus reminds us to be thankful.**

Another way we practice thankfulness is intentionally thanking at least one person every day. Who has served you? Who has helped you? Who do you depend on for support? Who has been kind, generous, and gracious to you? These are the people for whom we must say and show thanks. The lack of thankfulness is a sign we are consumed with self. The more we think about God and others, the more we will be reminded by the Spirit to be thankful. We thank God for you!

Reflection:

1. How do you express thankfulness?

2. How do you feel when others say thank you for something you've done or said?

3. Who can you show thanks to today? How will you do that?

Notes:

Action Step:
THANKS FOR GIVING

It's time to bake! Buy an easy to make cake, brownie, cookie, or dessert mix. Prepare and cook it together. Say three things you thank God for about one another. Take your dessert across the street to a neighbor and tell them a couple reasons your thankful God has them as your neighbor. Ask if you can pray for them or help them some way.

Our Prayer For You:

Jesus, thank you! You are the one we must remember to express gratitude with every day. It's because of your love, generosity, grace, and more that we are blessed. Help us remember to express thanks to everyone in our lives in a genuine way. As we rejoice and pray, may we be always thankful. In Jesus' name, Amen.

BE LOVING

Bible Verse:

"My command is this: Love each other as I have loved you."
                                                    –John 15:12

Something to Think About:

Everybody wants to be loved. Sometimes, we don't feel loved, but we must remember that God loves us with an unfailing love (Jeremiah 31:3). His love is immeasurable and expansive - wide, long, high, and deep (Ephesians 3:18-19). As we experience his love, we must give it away to others. There will be times you don't feel like loving others. So, Jesus instructed us to love based on His command and not our feelings. Love is a decision, not an emotion. While it involves our emotions, there may be times we don't feel like loving others. Even with a command, there is the choice not to obey it. That's why Jesus said we are to love each other "as I have loved you." When we are faced with the choice to love others, we must remember how Jesus has loved us and extend his love to others.

Truth to Treasure:

We should love others like Jesus loves us.

Most of the times when we don't want to love others it's because we have forgotten how much Jesus has forgiven us. Other times, we are not walking in his Spirit which leads to selfishness and insensitivity to the care of others. If we are to love "as Jesus has loved us", we must remember what this means. Jesus sacrificially gave his life for us. He was willing to die for us. He took on the weight of our sin, which was not his to bear. We were guilty, but he extended grace. He was selfless, not considering his own desires. Jesus was committed, forgiving, and merciful. He considered our best interest even when rejected by those he loved. When we love others like Jesus, we point them to Jesus. Loving others fulfills the command Jesus gave us. Obeying Him is an act of worship. You'll never go wrong when you love others as Jesus loved you.

Reflection:

1. Do you ever find it difficult to love others?

2. What does it mean to love others like Jesus loved?

3. Can you think of some practical ways to show Jesus' love to others?

Notes:

Action Step:

CARDS OF LOVE

Write an encouraging card to a relative, neighbor, or friend after you pray about who you believe God wants you to show love. Write a Bible verse of encouragement. List at least three things you love about that person. Write a statement reminding them that God loves them. Decorate it and mail it to them. What else could you include to show love?

Our Prayer For You:

Jesus, help me love others like you love us. I desire to obey your command to love others like you want them to be loved. Keep me from selfishness. I desire to extend grace, mercy, forgiveness, and compassion. Thank you for giving those to me. In Jesus' name, Amen.

BE JOYFUL

Bible Verse:

"Rejoice in the Lord always. I will say it again: rejoice!"
–Philippians 4:4

Something to Think About:

What makes you happy? Family? Friends? Here's another question: what makes you sad? Is it the same things when they go wrong? Happiness and sadness are often like riding a roller coaster - up and down with lots of twists and turns! Happiness is based on our circumstances. When they are good, we are good. When they aren't, we aren't. However, joy is something altogether different. Joy is based on Christ. We can have joy that comes from Christ no matter what our circumstances are. When the Apostle Paul wrote "rejoice in the Lord always" in Philippians 4:4, he was doing so in prison and possibly near the end of his life. What gave him joy in that bleak situation? Jesus!

Look at what Paul said again: "Rejoice IN THE LORD always." Where did his joy come from? Where was it based? In Jesus. How often did he Encourage us to rejoice in Christ? ALWAYS! This means whatever your circumstance, Jesus is the source of our joy.

Truth to Treasure:

Remember where your joy comes from: Jesus!

The word "rejoice" means "remember where your joy comes from". It was so vital for Paul that he repeated his instruction: "I will say it again: rejoice".

When you find yourself sad, remember Jesus. You will have "ups and downs" in your emotions, feelings, and thoughts. The way to reset is not found in doing something that makes you happy but in worshipping Jesus who makes you holy. He fulfills us long after the things that make us happy fade. Rejoice in Jesus! Our joy comes from a life lived in him.

Reflection:

1. Why do we often feel happy and sad?

2. How do we maintain our joy?

3. How can we have joy in the worst of circumstances?

Notes:

Action Step:

SPOT THE JOY

With a Post-It notepad in hand, walk around the house and place a note on something that brings you joy (i.e. picture of your family, Bible, plants, instrument). Once you have gone through every room and placed at least one not in each room, write down on each note why it gives you joy. Discuss if your responses are good or not. Use those notes as prayer cards.

Our Prayer For You:

Jesus, help me find joy in you always. Our circumstances will not always lead us to happiness. Joy is found in your presence (Psalm 16:11). Help me remember where my joy comes from. You are my joy. I want to trust in you for peace and contentment. Thank you for joy that does not fade away. In Jesus' name, Amen.

BE PATIENT

Bible Verse:

"Be still before the Lord and wait patiently for him; do not fret when people succeed in their ways, when they carry out their wicked schemes."
–Psalm 37:7

Something to Think About:

How good are you at being patient? Most people will say they often struggle with patience, yet it is a fruit of the Spirit. That means, we should display this quality in our lives. The key to that is walking in or by the Spirit of God. Spending time with the Lord and in his Word is where we learn to be patient. Patience is more than waiting. It's been said patience is the condition in which you wait. When you must wait for something, are you bothered? Do you complain? Does waiting cause you frustration or negativity? Or are you considerate, loving, and at peace?

One way to have patience in something is to pray. While you are waiting on an answer from God or for a situation to be resolved, don't just pray for that, pray for other things. We've found that patience and trust are connected. If we trust the Lord, we will ask him to work and move forward with doing and thinking other things. When we find ourselves

Truth to Treasure:
Impatience is a form of worry which is a lack of trust in God.

consumed with anxiety while waiting for God to move is when we are not practicing patience. Impatience is another form of worry which is a lack of trust in God. While this isn't merely saying stop thinking about what's making you impatient, in a sense, it is. Patience can be summed up by making your request known to God in prayer, surrendering the answer and timing to him, and moving forward in living out God's mission in the meantime. It's refusing to be consumed with the unknown in anxiety. We need only to "be still in the Lord" (Psalm 37:7). The psalm continues with "don't fret", "hope in the Lord", "be meek", "keep his way", and "seek peace" as things to do while we wait on the Lord.

Reflection:

1. How is your patience? What causes impatience in your life?

2. Instead of worry and anxiety, what else could you do while you wait on God?

3. What are you having trouble waiting on God for right now?

Notes:

Action Step:
THE PATIENT GAME
This game is like the quiet game. Sit across from your child. Without words or touch, try to make each other make a noise or talk. The first person to make any kind of sound loses. Sometimes, being patient requires sitting still and taming our tongues. After the game, talk about how hard it is to be patient sometimes and ways to help us be patient (pray, serve, praise, etc.).

Our Prayer For You:

Jesus, help us be patient. We desire to wait on you and trust you for the perfect answer and timing. When we are anxious, remind us how you've been faithful in the past. Remind us of your Word. You are timely and trustworthy. Thank you for your peace and comfort in the meantime. In Jesus' name, Amen.

BE KIND

Bible Verse:

"Anxiety weighs down the heart, but a kind word cheers it up."
                                                    –Proverbs 12:25

Something to Think About:

When you think of a kind person, who instantly comes to mind? Perhaps it's a good friend or a teacher you've had in school. There have been a lot of kind people in our lives, and we thank God for them. How do we know they were kind? They were very gracious and loving with their words and actions. None of us would call someone kind who was harsh with their words or rude with their actions. It means becoming a Psalm 19:14 person – "May the words of my mouth and the meditations of my heart be pleasing to You, Oh Lord, my Rock and my Redeemer". If the Lord isn't pleased with our words and actions, then they probably wouldn't be labeled by anyone else as kind.

A kind person is encouraging. People who have been kind to us over the years have helped us in difficult times by "bearing one another's burdens" (Galatians 6:2). Sometimes life gets hard, and you need people to help carry the burdens you face in life. A kind person does that! A kind person is an Ephesians 4:32 person – "Be kind and compassionate to one another, forgiving each other, just as in Christ God forgave you". They don't hold grudges because they remember how much Jesus has forgiven them. Remembering Jesus' forgiveness frees us to fully love someone from a heart of gratitude.

> *Truth to Treasure:*
> **Kind people do everything possible to reflect the nature of Jesus.**

You can describe the kindness of Christ with words like gentleness, compassionate, thoughtful, and generous. Kindness is a fruit of the Spirit (Galatians 5:22-23), so as you walk in the Spirit, He will make you more kind!

Reflection:

1. Who has shown you kindness to you lately?

2. What do you think keeps us from being kind?

3. Who can you show God's kindness to this week and how will you do that?

Notes:

Action Step:

BE KIND CARDS
Prepare cards with kind and unkind statements on them and place in a container. Have your child draw one out. Ask if the statement is kind or unkind and how they would fix it if it was unkind. Ask who they would show the kindness toward if a kind statement. Allow this to create more kind statements and actions that could be displayed.

Our Prayer For You:

Jesus, thank you for modeling kindness. Help us to reflect your kindness in everything we do. May our words and actions display generosity, compassion, and love. Keep us from being harsh, angry, boastful, greedy, or anything else that does not imitate Your kindness that others desperately need. In Jesus' name, Amen.

BE GOOD

Bible Verse:

"His master replied, 'Well done, good and faithful servant! You have been faithful with a few things; I will put you in charge of many things. Come and share your master's happiness!'" —Matthew 25:21

Something to Think About:

As your parents, one thing we tend to tell you before you go to school, to a friend's house, or somewhere without us is "Be good". We use the word "good" in a lot of ways. We describe food as good as well as someone's behavior. We also greet people by saying "Good evening". The word "good" has various uses in our English language. It has even more interpretations when it comes to character. Goodness is a fruit of the Spirit (Galatians 5:22-23) and should be present in every Christian's life. How can we ensure we are good?

To be good, we must know what good is. When the Bible speaks of being "good", it is referencing God's holiness. He is perfect and good in every way. We know this because Scriptures like Psalm 100:5 says, "For the Lord is good and his love endures forever; his faithfulness continues through all generations." If we are to be "good and faithful servants"

Truth to Treasure:
God is good and we should point people to His goodness.

(Matthew 25:21) of a good and faithful God, we must spend time learning about and living out his character. God's Word, through the help of the Holy Spirit, shapes how we think, speak, and act. Jesus said, "The good person out of the good treasure of his heart produces good, and the evil person out of his evil treasure produces evil, for out of the abundance of the heart his mouth speaks" (Luke 6:45). As we spend time with God, we become more like him. We should desire to be more like Jesus and imitate him in all his goodness (3 John 1:11). In everything you say and do, display the goodness of God!

Reflection:

1. Can you describe the goodness of God in a few words?

2. How can we display God's goodness to others?

3. What keeps us from displaying God's goodness?

Notes:

Action Step:

GOOD FRUIT BAD FRUIT
Pick a fruit that looks good on the outside but tastes bad on the inside (lemon, grapefruit, etc). Pick another fruit that looks bad on the outside but tastes good on the inside (perhaps a banana you use a sharpie to make black on the peel). Describe how goodness starts on the inside. It's not just about what we do, but who we are in Christ.

Our Prayer For You:

Jesus, you are good in every way. Help us to hate evil and cling to what is good. We must not withhold good from others but give it to whom it is due. We desire to imitate your goodness so others will see how good you are. Keep us from anything evil, even the appearance of evil. In Jesus' name, Amen.

BE FAITHFUL

Bible Verse:

"His master replied, 'Well done, good and faithful servant! You have been faithful with a few things; I will put you in charge of many things. Come and share your master's happiness!'" –Matthew 25:21

Something to Think About:

Another fruit of the Spirit is faithfulness. What does it mean to be faithful? Like all the fruits of the Spirit, they come from the Spirit of God. As God shapes our lives to be more like him in our character, we will display his faithfulness through our words and actions. To be faithful is to be loyal and steadfast. A faithful person can be counted on. They honor their commitments because their character can back up their promises. A faithful person is dependable and trustworthy. These are all qualities of Jesus. Matthew 25:21 says a servant of God is both good and faithful.

Faithfulness in God means there is evidence faith in God in our lives. It doesn't mean we will be perfect in our walk with God, but it does mean we will continue to trust and follow Him even when life becomes difficult and confusing. God is faithful to us. He will never leave or forsake us (Hebrews 13:5). This verse originates in Deuteronomy 31:6 with God's promise to Joshua. God said he would never leave him, but also commanded Joshua to be bold and courageous – a display of his faithfulness. Because God is faithful, we should also be faithful.

Truth to Treasure:
Because God is faithful, we should also be faithful.

Faithfulness is expressed through our relationships. We should be faithful to our church family. We should be faithful to our spouses, parents, children, friends, and even those we work with. One of the greatest God-like attributes you can be known by is to be faithful! Walk with the Spirit and faithfulness will be part of your life.

Reflection:

1. What does it mean to be faithful?

2. How has God been faithful to you?

3. In what area of life do you struggle with faithfulness?

Notes:

Action Step:

FAITHFUL SHIRTS

Buy an oversized white shirt and write the word "FAITHFULNESS" on it. Say, "Faithfulness is sticking together". Put two people in the same shirt and attempt to do common activities around the house together like water the plants, feed the dog, vacuum the floor, pick up toys, etc. How is faithfulness challenging? How is it rewarding?

Our Prayer For You:

Jesus, thank you for your faithfulness. You were sent by God to die on the cross and you faithfully died in our place for our sins. You kept your word in all ways. Your promises are always true. Help us to be faithful like you. As we walk in the Spirit, produce faithfulness in our lives. In Jesus' name, Amen.

BE GENTLE

Bible Verse:

"Let your gentleness be evident to all. The Lord is near."
—Philippians 4:5

Something to Think About:

Of all the fruit of the Spirit, gentleness may seem "the easiest". Judging the fruit of the Spirit on a scale of easy/hard is probably not the best way to look at them. Without the Spirit, none of the fruit are possible. The Spirit's presence, filling, prompting, conviction, and more help us "walk by the Spirit". Walking reminds us this is a "step by step" journey. If we rush, we won't be able to understand if we are being gentle or harsh. As we look at one step, let's say our last conversation with someone, we can assess if we demonstrated the gentleness of God. Then, we can look at another step, let's say our interaction with the teller at the bank or our teacher at school, we can recall the smallest of details like our facial expressions, hand gestures, and even our eye movement and ask the Spirit to show us if we are gentle or not.

Truth to Treasure:

A grateful praying person is a gentle person.

Philippians 4:5 says we should let our gentleness be evident to all. This means obvious. No one should wonder if we are gentle because they know we are. They shouldn't worry if we will "blow up" on them, brush them off, or cause them anxiety. How do we do this? One key to understanding Scripture is to look at it in context. So, part of doing this is reading the verses around a verse. The verse before Philippians 4:5 says, "Rejoice in the Lord always, and again I say rejoice" (4:4). Thankfulness is a real key to gentleness! The verse after says, "Be anxious for nothing, but in every situation, pray…" (4:6). Another key to gentleness is prayer! A grateful praying person is a gentle person. All this leads to a peaceful person (4:7). Practice gentleness by walking slowly in the Spirit. Pray often. Thank God for everything!

Reflection:

1. What robs you of your gentleness?

2. What feeds your gentleness?

3. Is there a certain time, place, or person with whom you are less gentle?

Notes:

Action Step:

EGG RACE
Create an obstacle course in which you will carry an egg on a spoon in your mouth through. Describe gentleness during this exercise. See who can go the fastest, race to beat your previous time, or simply do the activity at the same time with your child to illustrate how we must display God's gentleness in our lives even in the craziest obstacles of life.

Our Prayer For You:

Jesus, help us display your gentleness in all areas of our lives. We want others to know us as gentle people. You are gentle and lowly, and we want to learn from you (Matthew 11:28-30). Help me walk slowly with your Spirit. Show me what steals and feeds my gentleness. Thank you for always being near. In Jesus' name, Amen.

BE SELF-CONTROLED

Bible Verse:
"No temptation has overtaken you that is not common to man. God is faithful, and he will not let you be tempted beyond your ability, but with the temptation he will also provide the way of escape, that you may be able to endure it." ‑1 Corinthians 10:13

Something to Think About:

One of the seemingly hardest fruits of the Spirit to "master" is self-control. That's because we are mostly super aware when we are out of control in sin and disobedience to God. When we repeatedly commit sin, it can discourage and cause us to think we will never be able to overcome and obtain freedom. Self-control is not "harder" than any other of the fruit from God's Spirit. It, like the others, requires spending time with the Lord and learning from him. Self-control is being Spirit-controlled. We must allow God's Spirit to lead, correct, and fill us. To be Spirit-controlled is to obey the Scripture instead of our flesh. The Spirit will guide us to his truth and strengthen us to say no to sin and yes to him and live self-controlled lives!

The Bible gives hope that self-control is within our reach. Not only is it a promised fruit of the Spirit, we can overcome our flesh when we are tempted. First Corinthians 10:13 says, "No temptation has overtaken you that is not common to man. God is faithful, and he will not let you be tempted beyond your ability, but with the temptation he will also provide the way of escape, that you may be able to endure it." Did you catch that? Temptation to sin is something all believers face. But there is good news. God is faithful. He is dependable. He is in control! He gives us a way out. This means we can say no to sin and our selfish flesh and yes to obeying him. It's kind of like having an escape hatch or emergency exit on a bus when it is on fire. We must use the exit strategy God provides and exercise self-control over sin before we are consumed by it. Allow God's Spirit to lead you and control you.

Truth to Treasure:
Self-control is being Spirit-controlled.

Reflection:

1. What part of your feels out of control?

2. How do we all the Spirit to control us?

3. What sin constantly keeps returning to your life and what are your escape hatches?

Notes:

Action Step:

FREEZE DANCE
Pick a playlist of your child's favorite upbeat songs. Explain that as you play the songs, you should dance, but when the song pauses, you must freeze until the song resumes. Have fun with this and see how long it takes for someone to move before the song starts back. Discuss self-control during your pauses.

Our Prayer For You:

Jesus, thank you for giving us a way out of sin. Thank you for the hope you give through the Spirit's presence in our lives. Help us to obey your Word and trust that you have the best plan for our lives. When we are tempted, help us see the escape hatch you provide so we can live a Spirit-controlled life. In Jesus' name, Amen.

BE HUMBLE

Bible Verse:

"Humble yourselves, therefore, under God's mighty hand, that He may lift you up in due time."   -1 Peter 5:6

Something to Think About:

Who do you think of when you hear the word humility? What does humility mean? Humility is the opposite of pride. Scripture says pride goes before destruction and a haughty spirit before a fall (Proverbs 16:18). There are several characteristics of a humble person. They exhibit the fruit of the Spirit (Galatians 5:22-23). A humble person isn't arrogant, boastful, or rude. They do not seek attention for themselves. Philippians 2:3 says, "Do nothing out of selfish ambition or vain conceit. Rather, in humility, value others above yourselves."

Jesus is our greatest example of humility. Philippians continues and says Jesus, "made himself nothing by taking on the nature of a servant…he humbled himself by becoming obedient to death, even death on a cross" (2:7-8). Jesus willingly died on the cross for our sins. While being fully God, Jesus became fully human to die for our sins. The cross was a torture device meant for criminals. Jesus went through pain and suffering because he loved us. He humbly gave his life for our salvation.

Truth to Treasure:
Jesus is our greatest example of humility.

The world around us constantly reminds us to put ourselves first and do whatever makes us happy. True contentment and joy are found in serving others like Jesus did and helping others find a relationship with Jesus. We must be humble by "not looking to our own interests but to the interests of others" (Philippians 2:4). Whatever you do, walk in humility like Jesus.

Reflection:

1. Describe the qualities of someone you know that is humble?

2. Is it easy to spot pride and humility in someone else's life? What about yours?

3. How is Jesus' death our greatest example of humility?

Notes:

Action Step:

TRASH PICKUP
Go to a public place and pick up trash. Take trash bags, gloves, and even a tool to help collect trash. While you collect trash, discuss this phrase about humility: Serving others by giving up something you think you deserve and putting them first.

Our Prayer For You:

Jesus, thank you for your humility. You considered our sins and willingly died in our place. Thank you for forgiveness. Help me display your humility to others in my life. Help me be mindful of other's and humbly consider them before myself. I desire others to see you in my life. In Jesus' name, Amen.

BE GRACIOUS

Bible Verse:

"The Lord is gracious and compassionate, slow to anger and rich in love. The Lord is good to all; he has compassion on all he has made."
–Psalm 145:8-9

Something to Think About:

Extending God's grace to others only happens when you have experienced His grace. Being gracious can be interpreted as being courteous, but it is more than that. All of us should have and use good manners with others, but that is also not fully what it means to be gracious. Being gracious doesn't originate from outward actions, but from inward change. It reflects God's grace that's been poured out in your life.

Grace has been defined as God's unmerited favor or blessing on your life. It is how God has displayed his goodness to us with an understanding of how we don't deserve it. Psalm 145:8 says, "The Lord is gracious and compassionate, slow to anger and rich in love." His expression of grace towards us is only possible because of his character – he is slow to anger and rich in love. Grace is based on character. When we have experienced the genuine nature of God's perfect character, we should desire to become more like him in every way. As he changes our character, we can respond to people with His grace because it is present in our lives.

Truth to Treasure:
Being gracious originates from the inside, not the outside.

God's greatest gift of grace is salvation. Ephesians 2:8 says, "We have been saved by grace through faith". God's grace saves us and changes our attitude, actions, words, thoughts, and passions. If we want to be like God – "gracious, compassionate, slow to anger, and rich in love", then we must spend time with him and let him change us by His grace.

Reflection:

1. What does it mean to be gracious?

2. Would others consider you gracious, compassionate, slow to anger, and rich in love?

3. How has God's grace helped you grow in each of these areas?

Notes:

Action Step:

THE GRACE RACE
Write down the letters of GRACE on five separate pieces of paper and tape them on the walls in five different rooms of your house. Hide them good! As you race to find each letter, read five Bible Verses with the word GRACE in them. Ephesians 2:8, 2 Timothy 1:9, John 1:16, Titus 2:12, and Acts 15:11.

Our Prayer For You:

Jesus, thank you for your extending your grace into our lives. Your grace brings salvation and help us to reflect your character to others. Help us be gracious, compassionate, slow to anger, and rich in love. We desire to display your grace in every area of our lives. In Jesus' name, Amen.

BE FORGIVING

Bible Verse:

"Bear with each other and forgive one another if any of you have a grievance against someone. Forgive as the Lord forgave you."
—Colossians 3:13

Something to Think About:

Have you ever owed a debt you could not pay? Maybe you've broken something and you didn't have the money to repair or replace it. When I (mom) was in high school, I got a credit card at the store where I worked. I used the card to buy clothes and didn't keep track of my spending. My summer job was over, and I was headed to college with debt on the credit card I couldn't pay. My mom was merciful and paid the debt in full. That helped me learn a lesson about forgiveness.

In Matthew 18:21-35, Jesus told a parable about a man owed 20 years of wages to a king. The king asked him to pay, and he couldn't. The man asked for mercy and more time to pay. Instead, the king forgave everything he owed. After that, the man found one of his servants who owed him a day's wage. That man's servant also asked for mercy and more time to pay. Instead of forgiving, he choked him, demanded his money, and threw him into prison. When the king heard about this, he was angry and asked him why he didn't forgive the debt like he had been forgiven. The king then ordered the unmerciful servant to be thrown into prison until he could pay.

Truth to Treasure: **We should forgive others like Jesus forgave us.**

This parable from Jesus teaches us how we must forgive because of how much we have been forgiven. It's so easy to hold a grudge or allow unforgiveness to control us. We should be like the king, who represents Jesus in the story, and forgive. How can we allow unforgiveness to go on when we have been forgiven by Jesus from so much? Be like Jesus – be forgiving!

Reflection:

1. In the parable, who does the king and his servant represent? What about the one who owed the king's servant?

2. How is it possible to forgive someone who has hurt us so bad?

3. Do you have any unforgiveness or bitterness towards someone?

Notes:

Action Step:

BAG OF ROCKS
Get a backpack and some rocks. Discuss how we become angry and become bitter or seek revenge. Unforgiveness is like carrying a bag of rocks on our back. As you place rocks in the backpack, have them walk around while describing bitterness, anger, rage, revenge, etc. Now, have them say, "I will forgive" several times and each time they do, remove a rock.

Our Prayer For You:

Jesus, thank you for forgiving us from all our sin. Help us to forgive others in the same manner you forgive us. Help us to be like you in this parable: merciful, gracious, and kind. Keep us from being like the unmerciful servant. Bring to memory anyone I may have not forgiven so I can do that. In Jesus' name, Amen.

BE GENEROUS

Bible Verse:

"Each of you should give what you have decided in your heart to give, not reluctantly or under compulsion, for God loves a cheerful giver."
-2 Corinthians 9:7

Something to Think About:

God has given us so much. He has given us life, salvation, family, friends – everything! When we are generous, we are like God. One of the most familiar verses in the Bible says, "For God so loved the world that he gave His one and only Son…" (John 3:16). God is our definition and example of generosity. In 2 Corinthians 9:7, Paul told the church to "give what you have decided in your heart to give". Giving starts in our hearts. Whether it is time, service, money, or something else, whatever we give to someone else must be done from a right heart.

Paul continued in verse 7 by telling us about the character behind our giving. He said we are to give "not reluctantly or under compulsion". We are not generous because of guilt or force. That wouldn't be freely given. That would be someone taking from us. We give because we want to give. The reason we give is more important that what we give. We may give everything we have to help someone, but if we do it out of reluctance, guilt, or with intentions of receiving something in return, it is for the wrong reason.

Truth To Treasure:

Generosity starts in the heart.

We must give freely – because we desire to give. We must also give as a way to worship God, not get something in return. Whatever we give, it must be with an attitude of worship unto God. When we receive, we must be thankful to the person who gave and to God. We must remember God is the one who gives everything (2 Corinthians 9:10) and be a channel of his generosity to others.

Reflection:

1. What is generosity?

2. In what ways can we be generous?

3. How do we maintain the right heart when it comes to generosity?

Notes:

Action Step:

GENEROUS DONATIONS

When we were moving, we made a donate and sell pile. What could you donate to someone in need? What could you sell so you will have money to donate to a homeless shelter, food pantry, recovery ministry, etc.? We may not have cash on hand to donate (maybe you do), but stuff can work the same if we get creative and generous. This helps us learn sacrificial generosity.

Our Prayer For You:

Jesus, thank you for your generosity. God, you gave us Jesus to forgive us from sin. Thank you for your grace, compassion, provision, and love. Help us be generous with our words, actions, money, and possessions. We desire to be a blessing to others and worship you in all our giving. In Jesus' name, Amen.

BE COMPASSIONATE

Bible Verse:

"This is how we know what love is: Jesus Christ laid down his life for us. And we ought to lay down our lives for our brothers and sisters."
—1 John 3:16

Something to Think About:

When someone is having a bad day, how do you respond? If they are sick, hurting, depressed, or struggling with something, are you sympathetic or apathetic? Compassion is something we all need and should offer others. Compassion is love expressed. Jesus expressed his love and compassion to us, and we should do the same towards others. 1 John 3:16-18 helps us understand Jesus' compassion. Verse 16 says, "Jesus Christ willingly laid down his life for us, and we ought to lay down our lives for our brothers and sisters." This verse implies because Jesus did this, we should respond to his selflessness by being compassionate toward others.

How do we do this practically? Verse 17 says, "If anyone has material possessions and sees his brother and sister in need but has no pity on them, how can the love of God be in that person?" If we ignore or are indifferent to someone in need, we do not show the compassion of Christ to them.

Truth to Treasure:

Compassion is love expressed.

Compassion includes giving time, words, a listening ear, and even money to someone in need. Verse 18 continues, "Dear children, let us not love with words or speech but with actions and in truth." This doesn't mean we shouldn't say encouraging things to those in need. It means we should do more than just say we have compassion – we must show we have compassion.

God will show you opportunities this week to show compassion to others. Remember to do it with the love of Christ. When you do, it is worship to God and helps point people to God.

Reflection:

1. According to Jesus, who is your neighbor?

2. When should we love our neighbors?

3. From reading about the Good Samaritan (Luke 10:25-37), what does it mean to "show mercy" and "go and do likewise"?

Notes:

Action Step:

NECESSITY BAGS
Think about how you could serve someone in a nursing home, hospital, or the homeless. Perhaps providing basic necessity kits with toiletries, snacks, poncho, chapstick, wipes, socks, etc. Maybe you could volunteer one day in a food pantry. Maybe start with taking food to your local food pantry. There are many great ways to show compassion to others.

Our Prayer For You:

Jesus, thank you for reminding us to love God and love our neighbors. Help us to remember those two principles go together at all times. Help us love our neighbor through showing mercy and compassion. When someone has a need, we must be willing to stop whatever we are doing and help them in the name of Jesus. Amen.

BE A GOOD NEIGHBOR

Bible Verse:
"Love the Lord your God with all your heart and with all your soul and with all your strength and with all your mind and love your neighbor as yourself." -Luke 10:27

Something To Think About:

Whether you live in the city or a more rural area, everyone has neighbors. We know some of them better than others, and some we don't know at all. As a kid, I heard a story in the Bible Jesus gave about loving your neighbor. Two religious people passed up the hurt Jewish man, but one man, a Samaritan, stopped and helped. What confused me about the story was, according to my definition of a neighbor as a person who lived next door to me, the hurt Jewish man and the Samaritan who helped him didn't live on the same street. In fact, Jews and Samaritans didn't associate in that day. So just who is my neighbor that I'm supposed to love?

Jesus was telling the story to Jewish religious leaders. When Jesus gave them Scripture they knew (Deut. 6:4-9; Lev.19:18), one of them asked, "Who is my neighbor?" That was my question! The story proved my "neighbor" who needed love was whomever was in need. It doesn't matter if I live next door to them or know them well, we are to love everyone with Christ's love because he loves everyone! The Samaritan is not called "good" in the story, but that's how we know him. He showed the goodness of God through giving time, care, money, and whatever needed to the Jewish man in need – his neighbor.

Truth To Treasure:
Whoever needs Christ's love is my neighbor.

Jesus ended the story with the religious leaders by asking, "Who was his neighbor?" The Jewish leader replied, "The one who had mercy on him" (Luke 10:36). Jesus replied, "Go and do likewise" (v. 37). We must show mercy and do like the good Samaritan in the story.

Reflection:

1. According to Jesus, who is your neighbor?

2. When should we love our neighbors?

3. From reading about the Good Samaritan (Luke 10:25-37), what does it mean to "show mercy" and "go and do likewise"?

Notes:

Action Step:

SERVANT EVANGELISM
How well do you know your neighbors? Think about them and choose one you will practically serve this next week. It could be yard work, bake them something, wash their car/windows, or something else they need. Steve Sjogren offers great resources on servant evangelism ideas www.stevesjogren.com.

Our Prayer For You:

Jesus, thank you for reminding us to love God and love our neighbors. Help us to remember those two principles always go together. Help us love our neighbor through showing mercy and compassion. When someone has a need, we must be willing to stop whatever we are doing and help them in the name of Jesus. Amen.

BE AND MAKE DISCIPLES

Bible Verse:

"Therefore, go and make disciples of all nations, baptizing them in the name of the Father and of the Son and of the Holy Spirit."
-Matthew 28:19

Something to Think About:

Jesus calls us to be and make disciples. While we need time alone with the Lord, we don't need to wait a long time after being saved before we are able to start making disciples. When we learn something new in Christ, we should turn around and pass it along. When God shows us something in His Word, we are to share it with someone else. From the first day we are saved, we can start helping others grow in Christ. When we brought you home from the hospital, we didn't wait to start parenting when you turned one. We started on day one! We didn't know much, and we didn't have much experience, but God was with us every step of the way! As we learned to be husband and wife, we put it into practice on day one, not a few years later. The same is true with making disciples. As we grow in Jesus, we grow with others as disciples.

Truth to Treasure:
To be a disciple, I must also make disciples.

Discipleship simply comes down to obeying Jesus' instructions to the first disciples in Matthew 4:17. He said, "Come follow me, and I will make you fishers of men." There are three statements of discipleship here. First, we must follow Him. To follow Jesus means we submit all of who we are to all of who He wants us to be. It means we crucify the flesh (Galatians 5:24), obey His Word (John 14:15), and submit to God (James 4:7). Second, He makes us. We become new creations in Christ when we are saved (2 Corinthians 5:17). We are crucified in Christ and live in Him (Galatians 2:20). Matthew 4:17 ends by saying we are to be fishers of men. The mission of our lives is to glorify God, share the Gospel, and help others grow in Christ. As you follow Jesus, let him make you more into his image and, then pass that along to others.

Reflection:

1. Why are being and making disciples connected?

2. Why do we often wait to pass on what we learn in our walk with Christ?

3. Who comes to mind as someone you can help disciple in the Lord?

Notes:

Action Step:

DISCIPLE REMINDERS
Make an "I AM A DISCIPLE" bracelets to remind one another of discipleship. You can buy bracelet kits online. Be creative! You can also make disciple notecards and place them around the house (mirror, desk, refrigerator, etc.). Write the Great Commission (Matthew 28:19-20), discipleship goals, memory verses, prayer requests, etc. on them.

Our Prayer For You:

Jesus, thank you for calling us to follow you and giving us your command to make disciples. Help us to pass on what we learn from you to someone else so they can also grow closer to you. Thank you for the opportunity to grow with other as your disciples. In Jesus' name, Amen.

BE A WITNESS

Bible Verse:

"That which was from the beginning, which we have heard, which we have seen with our eyes, which we have looked at and our hands have touched–this we proclaim concerning the Word of life." -1 John 1:1

Something to Think About:

Have you ever witnessed something so spectacular that you had to share it with someone else? We've witnessed some incredible things like the beauty of the Hawaiian Islands and the launch of a space shuttle in Florida. Nothing compares to experiencing firsthand the miracles of your birth. God's creation of tiny humans inside your mom's belly is something almost too wonderful to imagine. To top it off, watching you grow every day since has been something we love telling others about. When the Apostle John wrote 1 John, he began by saying about Jesus, "What we have heard…seen…looked at and our hands have touched, this we proclaim" (v. 1). A witness talks about their experience of something. What better to share than one's experience in Christ!

Truth to Treasure: *The best thing you could share with someone is Jesus.*

Acts 1:8 says God gives us the power of the Holy Spirit to be his witnesses. The good news is we don't have to be experts or the most eloquent with words. We simply share the good news of the gospel and God's Word along with our experiences as we follow Jesus. The Holy Spirit will empower us with the words to say and the boldness to share. Like John, we can testify to others about our lives in Christ and this can give us great joy (1 John 1:4). Witnessing to others is more about telling others about Jesus from an overflow of love for him rather than attempting to be persuasive to make them do something. As you grow in Jesus, talk about it with others. As you read God's Word, testify of how he has changed your life. As you are God's witness in everyday life and conversation, you'll discover the great joy it will bring to you. Tell others about Jesus – there's nothing greater!

Reflection:

1. What have you experienced in your walk with Jesus that you could share with someone else?

2. Why do we sometimes hesitate to share about Jesus with others?

3. Who do you know that needs to hear something encouraging or helpful from your witness of following Jesus?

Notes:

Action Step:

SALVATION ABCs

God wants us to share the gospel with others. Teach your child the ABCs of the gospel. A – Admit you are a sinner (Romans 3:23; 6:23); B – Believe Jesus can save (John 3:16); C – Confess your sins (Romans 10:9-10, 13). Practice this with one another. Pray for a friend they can share the ABCs with. Plan a time to share the ABCs with them.

Our Prayer For You:

Jesus, thank you for allowing us to share you with others. What we read in your Word and experience from following you can help lead others closer to you. Thank you for giving us your Holy Spirit to be your witnesses. Give us boldness to share the overflow of our love for you with others! In Jesus' name, Amen.

BE SEXUALLY PURE

Bible Verse:

"Above all else, guard your heart, for everything you do flows from it." -Proverbs 4:23

Something to Think About:

(Use discretion and wisdom when you believe your child is old enough for this lesson). It is God's desire that we be holy as he is holy. That's a Scripture we are to live out (1 Peter 1:16). Purity is something that starts in our thoughts. Our external actions are a reflection and reaction to our internal desires. This is why Solomon said in Proverbs 4:23 "Above all else, guard your heart, for everything you do flows from it." There is a battle for your purity, and it's won or lost in the mind. Temptation to do impure or unholy sinful actions is something we all face. As an example, God created sex to be a blessing for a man and a woman in marriage. Sexual impurity (sin) happens when we remove it from or distort it in marriage. When we do things the way God designed, we will then have his blessing and find the greatest joy.

Truth to Treasure:

The battle for purity is won or lost in the mind.

Impure actions begin with impure thoughts. We usually allow a dumb thought to turn into a dumb action. God helps us overcome wrong thoughts which can become wrong actions by obeying his Word. 2 Timothy 2:22 says, "Flee the evil desires of youth and pursue righteousness, faith, love and peace, along with those who call on the Lord out of a pure heart." We must not entertain evil desires. We must run from them. At the same time, we must run toward the things of God. This Scripture says pursue "those who call on the Lord out of a pure heart". We must hang around people who desire to be holy and stay away from those who would tempt us to do wrong. As you pursue purity, remember to pursue the Lord. He's the goal. He can and will keep us from a life of unholiness and sin. We can be fully satisfied in a life that is spent pursuing Jesus.

Reflection:

1. Why is guarding our hearts so important?

2. How do pursuing God and fleeing sin go hand in hand?

3. Who defines purity?

Notes:

Action Step:

PURITY WEEKEND

When your kids are the appropriate age (I suggest somewhere around 10-13), take them on a weekend trip alone and go through a sexual purity curriculum such as *Passport 2 Purity* by Family Life. *The Talk* (Gilkerson) is also a good book resource. Above all, pray and engage your children biblically at the right time.

Our Prayer For You:

Jesus, thank you helping us pursue you. You give us strength to overcome the temptation to sin. Help me see sex as something you created wonderfully for marriage. Help me pursue you and relationships that honor you. Give me wisdom to flee sin. Give me a pure heart and mind. In Jesus' name, Amen.

BE CONTENT

Bible Verse:

"But godliness with contentment is great gain."   -1 Timothy 6:6

Something to Think About:

Are you satisfied with what you have? Do you ever feel "more" of something will make you happier? Contentment can be elusive. The feeling of never being satisfied and fulfilled can overwhelm you even if you have every reason to be satisfied and fulfilled. The Apostle Paul understood and achieved contentment in life. He says in Philippians 4:12-14, "I am not saying this because I am in need, for I have learned to be content whatever the circumstances. I know what it is to be in need, and I know what it is to have plenty. I have learned the secret of being content in any and every situation, whether well fed or hungry, whether living in plenty or in want. I can do all this through him who gives me strength."

We tend to think if we can get more, then we'll be content. Contentment is not something we get. It's something we're given. Jesus fills our lives with peace, joy, meaning and so much beyond what possessions or achievements in this world could.

Truth to Treasure:
Contentment is not something we get. It's something we're given.

Contentment is a biblical principle and discipline that every Christ follower should seek. Paul was content with weakness for the sake of Christ (2 Corinthians 12:10). Paul told Timothy that godliness with contentment is great gain (1 Timothy 6:6). He even said if he had food and clothing, that would be enough (1 Timothy 6:8). The only thing that can bring us true contentment in this life is a relationship with Jesus. We must learn to rest in God's provision and presence. He is enough. Only God can quiet and calm our restlessness. If you find yourself discontent, ask God to give you more of Himself. Only He can truly satisfy our greatest desires.

Reflection:

1. What brings you true happiness and fulfillment?

2. Have you learned to be content whatever the circumstances?

3. Would you be satisfied only having the basic necessities? Why or why not?

Notes:

Action Step:
CONTENTMENT ROCKS
Read Joshua 4:21-24. Joshua set up a pillar of stones so Israel would remember all God had done for them. Find a smooth stone and write "contentment" on it with a permanent marker, nail polish, or paint. Decorate it if you want. Use it as a reminder in your home to remember all God has done for you and be thankful for all he has given you.

Our Prayer For You:

Jesus, thank you for giving us contentment. I know if I worked all my life, I could never get enough to be happy and at peace. You alone satisfy my deepest desires. Thank you for giving me peace, joy, and purpose. Help me learn the secret of being content just like the Apostle Paul. In Jesus' name we pray, Amen.

SPIRITUAL WARFARE

Bible Verse:

"For our struggle is not with flesh and blood but with the principalities, with the powers, with the world rulers of this present darkness, with the evil spirits in the heavens." -Ephesians 6:12

Something to Think About:

There are a lot of military-like video games that simulate real war scenarios. As good as graphics have become, they still do not compare to the reality of battle. Many wars have been fought for thousands of years on different fronts, with different weapons, for different reasons. Some of those battles are mentioned in the Bible (read Joshua, Judges, 1 & 2 Samuel, 1 & 2 Kings). There is a type of warfare that isn't fought with physical weapons or armies. Spiritual warfare is real and mentioned several times in Scripture.

Paul told us, "For our struggle is not with flesh and blood but with the principalities, with the powers, with the world rulers of this present darkness, with the evil spirits in the heavens" (Ephesians 6:12). He continued by mentioning the armor of God we use – shield of faith, helmet of salvation, breastplate of righteousness, belt of truth, gospel shoes, sword of the Spirit, and prayer.

Truth To Treasure:
God has given us everything we need to overcome the evil one.

We use God's Word, prayer, faith, and other spiritual weapons to combat a real enemy – the devil. Peter says, "Be sober and vigilant. Your opponent the devil is prowling around like a roaring lion looking for someone to devour" (1 Peter 5:8). You're in a battle with the devil who is a liar, manipulator, and tempter, so be alert! We are under attack, but don't worry. Jesus conquered the grave and is victoriously seated at God's right hand. He even prays for us! We have God's Spirit in us. We have everything we need to overcome the enemy. "Submit yourself to God. Resist the devil, and he will flee from you" (James 4:7). "Greater is he that is in you than he that is in the world" (1 John 4:4).

Reflection:

1. How do you know you are being spiritually attacked?

2. What is your favorite spiritual weapon listed in Ephesians 6?

3. How does Jesus' resurrection give you confidence in spiritual warfare?

Notes:

Action Step:

EGG PROTECTION

Do this activity outside. Place an egg in the palm of your hand and squeeze. The egg is protected from the pressure by the shell. Discuss the pieces of the Armor of God in Ephesians 6. What happens if the eggshell is cracked or removed (i.e. shield of faith, breastplate of righteousness, helmet of salvation are removed from our lives)?

Our Prayer For You:

Jesus, thank you for overcoming the devil through your resurrection. You did not leave us defenseless against satan's attacks. Thank you for the Spirit of God that lives in us and the Word that is sharper than any two-edged sword (Hebrews 4:12). Help us submit to you and resist the devil. In Jesus' name we pray, Amen.

REPENTANCE

Bible Verse:

"From that time on Jesus began to preach, "Repent, for the kingdom of heaven has come near."

-Matthew 4:17

Something to Think About:

When Jesus began his ministry on earth, his first sermon was "Repent, for the kingdom of heaven has come near" (Matthew 4:17). Repentance was so important that he started his ministry with it! Repentance is not just feeling sorry or having regret for doing something wrong. We can have those and never change. The word repentance means "to change one's mind". When we repent, we are admitting we were wrong and God is right, allowing God to change our minds and actions, and asking God to help us never do that again. The motivation of this is desire to honor God with our lives and obey His Word.

The Apostle Paul tells us the difference between being sorry and repentance in 2 Corinthians 7:8-13. He wrote to the Corinthian believers about some sin they were involved in and asked them to repent. He said, "your sorrow led to repentance" (v. 9). He continued by saying "godly sorrow

Truth to Treasure:
Repentance brings encouragement and restoration with God.

brings repentance...but worldly sorrow brings death" (v. 10). He even listed several poofs of repentance (v. 11). He ends by saying repentance brings encouragement (v. 13). When we have true repentance, it encourages us and others that sin will not control us forever. There is freedom in Christ!

When you sin, allow the Holy Spirit to convict you of sin – that's one of his jobs (John 16:8). Thank God when we ask him to forgive us he will! He also cleanses us from all unrighteousness (1 John 1:9). Don't get stuck in sin. We have the gift of repentance to lead us back to Jesus.

Reflection:

1. Why do we sometimes delay or resist repentance?

2. When was the last time you knew you needed to repent and change?

3. Is there anything you need to repent of today?

Notes:

Action Step:

EMPTY SHOES

Plan a family walk. Place a small pebble or pea gravel in your child's shoe. Don't let them remove it too soon. After a few minutes, stop and clean out the shoes. The rock represents sin in our lives. How did it feel with the rock present and removed? "Emptying our shoes" or repentance helps focus on enjoying the journey instead of the painful rock.

Our Prayer For You:

Jesus, thank you for forgiving us when we ask. You empower us to change our minds, actions, and honor you with our lives. Help us to obey your message to repent of sin. We don't want worldly sorrow. We desire godly sorrow that leads to repentance. Thank you for drawing us back to you. In Jesus' name we pray, Amen.

YOUR IDENTITY IN CHRIST

Bible Verse:

"I have been crucified with Christ and I no longer live, but Christ lives in me. The life I now live in the body, I live by faith in the Son of God, who loved me and gave himself for me."   -Galatians 2:20

Something to Think About:

Have you ever had someone ask you, "Who are you?" We usually answer by giving our name and describing some things about ourselves (address, family, work, school, etc.). Here's a better question? Who are you in Christ? We have an identity in Christ. When we are saved, we become a new creation (2 Corinthians 5:17). While we may identify ourselves by individual characteristics to "be our own person" from a worldly perspective, now we have a new identity from a spiritual and eternal perspective. We share characteristics with others who are part of his family, the church. In Christ, all believers no longer live for ourselves, but for Christ. Paul said, "We live by faith in the Son of God" (Galatians 2:20). In Christ we are no longer known by our sin and past but by who God says we have become through Jesus.

Truth to Treasure:
We are who God says we are.

In Christ, we are redeemed (Col 1:14), loved (Jer 31:3), a child of God (1 Jn 3:1), forgiven (1 Pet 2:24), set apart (1 Pet 2:9), a saint (1 Cor 6:11), a temple of the Holy Spirit (1 Cor 6:19), co-laborers with God (1 Cor 3:9), washed clean (Is 1:18), adopted in God's family (Rom 8:15), wonderfully made (Ps 139:14), ministers of reconciliation (2 Cor 5:18), ambassadors for Christ (2 Cor 5:20), righteous (2 Cor 5:21) and so much more!

Some days, our flesh, the world, and even the devil will try to draw us back to who we were before Christ. Don't let them! We don't have to be who others think we should be. We don't compare ourselves to others. We discover who we are in Christ and live in the identity He gave us through salvation.

Reflection:

1. What are some characteristics of Christians?

2. What characteristics does the world use for identity?

3. Based on our identity in Christ, how are we to live?

Notes:

Action Step:

IDENTITY PORTRAITS
Spend a few minutes thinking about how God created you. Draw or paint a self-portrait and write a list of things that God says about you from Scripture (use the Scripture above to get started if you need to). Psalm 139:13-18 is a good Scripture to use. List hobbies, interests, talents, attributes, fun facts, and anything else you see God has gifted you with.

Our Prayer For You:

Jesus, thank you for making us brand new through salvation. Help us remember our identity is found in you. I desire to be known by who your Word says I am. Thank you for giving me eternal purpose. Help me live in a way that my life in Christ and points people to you. In Jesus' name we pray, Amen.

CONFLICT RESOLUTION

Bible Verse:

"Do not repay anyone evil for evil. Be careful to do what is right in the eyes of everyone. If it is possible, as far as it depends on you, live at peace with everyone."   -Romans 12:17-18

Something to Think About:

At some point, conflict will happen in every relationship. You can count on it. It even happens with the people we love the most. It may be minor and easily fixed, or it could be something that has potential to severely damage your relationship. How do we resolve conflict when it happens? One thing to remember is go after the problem and not the person. People are not our enemies. It's ok to have disagreement in our relationships. That only means we are different people! How we disagree is important. We should never remove the fruit of the Spirit from our times of disagreement. We must love those with whom we disagree. We must have patience as we attempt to work on our differences.

Truth to Treasure:
In conflict, go after the problem, not the person.

Hurt is also possible in our relationships. We must be kind toward others, even if they have hurt us. We should also not allow someone to continue to hurt us. People have the potential to hurt us…and we can hurt them as well. Paul reminds us in Romans 12 not to return evil for evil. That means if someone hurts you, don't try to hurt them in return. He encourages us to do what is right. You may thing paying them back is right, but he clarifies do what is right "in the eyes of everyone". Our hurt can cause us to hurt others. We are to "live at peace with everyone". So how do we resolve conflict when it comes? First, love them like Jesus would. Second, ask to meet with them to discuss your conflict and invite someone who can help you both repair your relationship. Third, forgive like Jesus would. Fourth, repent where you're wrong. Last, pray. It may not be solved in that meeting, but in time it can with the Spirit's help.

Reflection:

1. Why does conflict happen in relationships?

2. Why does conflict continue in relationships?

3. What are some wrong ways of handling conflict? Right ways?

Notes:

Action Step:

CONFLICT RESOLUTION STEPS

Practice these conflict resolution steps:
1) COOL OFF – How do you get calm? Read Ephesians 4:26
2) UNDERSTAND – What does the others person want/feel? Read James 1:19
3) SERVE – How can I love them. Read Philippians 2:2-3.

Practice by creating an imaginary conflict scenario.

Our Prayer For You:

Jesus, thank you for helping us restore relationships. You offer all the tools necessary: forgiveness, peace, patience, repentance, etc. Help me pursue peace with others. Help me love them like you would. Use whatever means necessary to promote unity and restoration for your glory. In Jesus' name we pray, Amen.

BIBLICAL MANHOOD

Bible Verse:

"When I was a child, I talked like a child, I thought like a child, I reasoned like a child. When I became a man, I put the ways of childhood behind me."
-1 Corinthians 13:11

Something to Think About:

There are two genders – male and female. In the beginning, God created it this way. Genesis 1:27 says, "So God created mankind in his own image, in the image of God he created them; male and female he created them." Being male can be defined with biological and physical facts distinct from being female, but there are biblical qualities that should be noted. How are men created in God's image, especially those born again, to live? What is their character to be like? How do they act? What defines a man biblically?

Paul said when he was a male child, he acted that way, but when he became an adult, he put away childish things (1 Corinthians 13:11). Part of biblical manhood is growing up into God's design for masculinity. It's more than (and probably doesn't include) external factors like who can grow the best beard or kill the biggest deer. A clear direction for men to grow into the image of Christ is found in 1 Corinthians 16:13. Paul said, "Be on the alert, stand firm in the faith, act like men, be strong. Let all that you do be done in love." To "be on the alert" is to be aware spiritually, conscious of God's will and the enemy's temptations. To "stand firm in the faith" is to grow in our relationship with Jesus. To "act like men" is to be reminded of God's role and responsibility of men shaped by Jesus – to act in a way that gives honor to Christ. To "be strong" is more than physical strength, but spiritually, on the Rock that is Jesus. To "let all you do be done in love" is living a life centered on the love of Jesus (i.e.1 Cor. 13:4-7). Biblical men are humble servants who look more like Jesus every day.

Truth to Treasure:
Biblical manhood is growing up in God's design for masculinity.

Reflection:

1. What does it mean to be a man biblically?

2. How does the world's perspective of a man differ than God's?

3. What are some other Scriptures that help us understand biblical manhood?

Notes:

Action Step:

BIBLICAL MANHOOD CEREMONY
Plan a ceremony by inviting other godly men (grandfather, uncle, pastor, etc.) to attend and speak into your son's life. Have them write letters, eat together, and discuss biblical manhood. Present them a boy's devotional, Bible, or journal. If your child is a girl, have them write an encouraging letter to their dad or brother with some Bible verses.

Our Prayer For You:

Jesus, thank you for creating men and women. We believe your design is best and gladly embrace your creation and plan. Thank you for helping us see the qualities of a man that is growing up in Christ. Thank you for setting the example of humility, servanthood, and love for us to follow. In Jesus' name we pray, Amen.

BIBLICAL WOMANHOOD

Bible Verse:

"Charm is deceptive, and beauty is fleeting; but a woman who fears the Lord is to be praised."

-Proverbs 31:30

Something to Think About:

God created men and women (Genesis 1:27; 5:2). Jesus confirms this in Matthew 9:4. While men and women are physically and biologically different, biblical manhood and womanhood are about the distinctive character and roles of men and women as defined by Scripture. Both biblical manhood and womanhood start with being born again (John 3:3). Men and women equal in value in God's eyes and responsibility to follow Jesus.

The Bible says a woman's worth comes from "your inner self, the unfading beauty of a gentle and quiet spirit, which is of great worth in God's sight" and not outward appearances or adornment like jewelry or clothing (1 Peter 3:3-4). This doesn't mean the Bible is against these. It means a woman's value is found in how God sees her and reflected by her growing Christlike character. Biblical womanhood is more than outward appearance and the ability to have children. Proverbs 31:30 says, "charm is deceptive, and beauty is fleeting, but a woman who fears the Lord is to be praised."

Truth to Treasure: **A woman's value comes from God and is shown in Christlike character.**

Men and women are created equal in Christ (Galatians 3:28) with unique roles in aspects of life like marriage (Ephesians 5:23-31). Both women and men reveal and reflect God's glory in similar and unique ways. It is a wonderful thing to know God created you male or female and to grow in biblical manhood and womanhood. This not only glorifies God most as creator but fulfills you most as his creation. Praise God, you are fearfully and wonderfully made (Psalm 139:14).

Reflection:

1. What does it mean to be a woman biblically?

2. How does the world's perspective of a woman differ than God's?

3. What are some other Scriptures that help us understand biblical womanhood?

Notes:

Action Step:

BIBLICAL WOMANHOOD CEREMONY
Plan a ceremony by inviting other biblical women (grandmother, aunt, pastor's wife, etc.) to attend and speak into your daughter's life. Have them write a letters, eat together, and discuss biblical womanhood. Present them a girl's devotional, Bible, or journal. If your child is a boy, have them write an encouraging letter to their mom or sister with Bible verses.

Our Prayer For You:

Jesus, thank you for creating men and women. We believe your design is best and gladly embrace your creation and plan. Thank you for helping us see the value and qualities of a woman. Thank you basing all of it in your love and design for us and help us reflect your glory as your creation. In Jesus' name we pray, Amen.

HOW TO SAY YES AND NO

Bible Verse:

"All you need to say is simply 'Yes' or 'No'; anything beyond this comes from the evil one."
-Matthew 5:37

Something to Think About:

There are a lot of things in this world to which you can say "yes". There are also a lot of things we should say "no" to. We should say no to sin and whatever is not the Lord's will. We should say yes to obeying God's Word. In Matthew 5, the beginning of Jesus' "Sermon on the Mount", he tells those listening to "let your yes be yes and your no be no". In context, Jesus is telling them when they say yes or no, be truthful no matter the situation. We should not use the Scripture in a way that takes advantage of others, compromises our integrity, or dishonors God.

When you say yes to something, you're making a commitment and should desire and plan to follow through with that obligation. Sometimes we can over commit with good intentions. In that case, communicate with others and ask for more time, grace, or the possibility of being released from that commitment. One way to give others a good "yes" is to also know when to say "no".

Truth to Treasure:
A good no will produce a better yes.

There are a few guidelines I use when saying yes and no to something. I ask, "Does it glorify God? Does it accomplish His will for my life? Is it distracting, compromising, tempting, or will it weaken my walk with Christ? Will it hurt others? Will it increase my obedience and walk with Christ." A good no will produce a better yes. Sometimes, "yes" and "no" are "not yet" so you can accomplish other commitments. Sometimes, we should say yes even if we do not feel like it. We all have limited time and resources. We cannot say yes to everything, and we should not say no to everything. God will give you wisdom and discernment to say yes or no and the ability to fulfill your commitment.

Reflection:

1. What have you said yes to that is proving difficult to keep doing? Why?

2. Why is limiting our "yes" and "no" to commitment important?

3. What do you need to say no to so what you've said yes to will improve?

Notes:

Action Step:

YES AND NO GAME

The goal of the game is to get you to say yes or no to questions. The questions normally receive yes or no answers, but instead you must give another answer. Parents, make a list of questions. Example: "Do you have any brothers?" Normally, they'd say yes or no. Instead, they could answer "2". Be creative and try your best to get them to say yes or no and the game is over.

Our Prayer For You:

Jesus, thank you for giving us Kingdom purpose. Help us say yes to your Word and will. Help us say no to sin and anything that compromises your Word and will or that would hurt others. Help us not waste our lives on things that do not matter in your Kingdom. Help our yes be yes and our no be no. In Jesus' name we pray,

LISTEN TO THE HOLY SPIRIT

Bible Verse:

"For those who are led by the Spirit of God are the children of God."

-Romans 8:14

Something to Think About:

Everyone wants to know they are making the right decision. The key to this is listening to and obeying God. How do we know what God is saying to us? We've heard a lot of people say, "The Lord told me" when it was their own desires or feelings that they were obeying. The sure way to know you are obeying the voice of the Holy Spirit is to obey the Word of God. The Bible is God's primary method of speaking to us. All Scripture is inspired by the Holy Spirit (2 Timothy 3:16). That Scripture also says God's Word is useful for teaching, correcting, doctrine, and instruction. God's Word will tell us His will. God's will is not a mystery. There are Scriptures that say, "it is God's will" (1 Thess 4:3, 5:18; 1 Peter 2:15).

Romans 8:14 says we are led by the Spirit of God. The Spirit of God lives inside of us to lead us closer to God and away from sin. Because the Spirit of God lives in other believers, God uses them to also speak into our lives. We must match their words with God's Word. If it contradicts God's Word, it is not the Spirit speaking to us. Several times in Scripture we see the phrase, "Let him who has ears hear what the Spirit is saying" (Mark 4:9; Rev 2:11). This is always in context with the Word that was just spoken by Jesus or God through one of his prophets in the Old Testament (Jeremiah 6:10; Ezekiel 12:2). The Spirit does not speak anything contrary to His Word. If you want to know if it is God's Spirit speaking to you, read His. Word, test you intuition or someone's advice by comparing it to God's Word. God wants you to know his voice (John 10:27). The more you spend time with Jesus in prayer and the Word, the more you'll know his voice.

Truth to Treasure:

We must listen to and be led by the Spirit.

Reflection:

1. How do you know you are hearing God's voice?

2. Why is it important to test everything with God's Word?

3. Do you think God is speaking something to you right now? How will you know it's Him?

Notes:

Action Step:

TUNE IN TO GOD

Read John 10:27. You'll need an analog radio (the kind with a dial and an antenna). Turn it on and talk about turning in or listening to God. Move the dial around and find clear and not so clear stations. Talk about how we tune into God (read our Bible, pray, listen to the Holy Spirit, go to church, etc.). Ask: How do we know we are hearing God's voice?

Our Prayer For You:

Jesus, thank you for communicating to us through prayer and your Word. We want to know your will and obey. Thank you for giving us the Bible so we can discern your voice and other's advice. Let us hear what your Spirit is saying so we can follow and honor you. In Jesus' name we pray, Amen.

GOD'S FAITHFULNESS

Bible Verse:

"If we are faithless, he remains faithful, for he cannot disown himself." -2 Timothy 2:13

Something to Think About:

One of the best qualities of God is his faithfulness. There are many faithful people in this world, but no one has ever been fully faithful. While others may let us down, we can be confident God never will. Faithfulness is more than what God does; it is who he is. He is the definition of faithful. God always keeps his promises. Many Scriptures confirm his faithfulness. Lamentations 3:22 says, "Because of the Lord's great love we are not consumed, for his compassions never fail. They are new every morning. Great is your faithfulness." Hebrews 10:23 says, "Let us hold unswervingly to the hope we profess, for he who promised is faithful."

There are times when we face difficulties, and it may seem as though God is distant. We may even question his faithfulness to us. Just because you cannot see him or may not sense he is working does not mean he isn't. God's character gives us confidence in his faithfulness. Deuteronomy 7:9 reminds us God is faithful and keeps his promises to those who love him and keep his commandments to a thousand generations. God's nature is trustworthy and loving. He is compassionate and full of mercy. He is all-powerful, all-knowing, and ever-present. We can rest confidently and trust in God he is working everything for his glory and our good.

Truth to Treasure:
Faithfulness is more than what God does, it is who he is.

When others are unfaithful, practice patience, grace, and forgiveness. Pray for them. Ask God to help make you more faithful. May it be a quality you grow in the rest of your life.

Reflection:

1. How has God been faithful to you?

2. In what way do you need God's faithfulness now?

3. How can we display God's faithfulness to others in practical ways?

Notes:

Action Step:

FAITH OF A WATER DROP

You'll need a penny, a cup of water, and a medicine dropper. Ask: How many drops of water will fit on the head of a penny? Get answers. Place one drop at a time on the penny. With each drop, say how God's been faithful. You'll be surprised how many drops will fit! The water drops "stick together". God's faithfulness will also surprise you. Each "faith drop" reminds us He is faithful.

Our Prayer For You:

Jesus, thank you for always being faithful. Your character gives us confidence you will provide for us the best way you see fit. Help us to trust you when we cannot see you working. Help us to display your faithfulness to others in everything we say and do. In Jesus' name we pray, Amen.

GOD'S CHARACTER

Bible Verse:

""There is no one holy like the Lord; there is no one besides you. There is no Rock like our God."
-1 Samuel 2:2

Something to Think About:

God's character is perfect. That's because he is God. There are many perfect qualities about God that should bring us great peace and confidence in our relationship with him. Let's discuss how God is good, holy, and just. God is good and does good things (Psalm 119:68). There is nothing evil or threatening about his nature. We can trust him because of how good he is in his character. His works out all things to our good and his glory (Romans 8:28). Thank God for his goodness.

God is also holy. He is perfect in every way. 1 John 1:5 says, "God is light, and in him there is no darkness at all". This means there is no sin, evil, unrighteousness, or injustice with God. He is pure in his thoughts, choices, and actions. He cannot tolerate sin and his holiness required punishment for it through his sinless son Jesus' death on the cross. His goodness will never conflict with his holiness. Thank God for his holiness.

Truth to Treasure:
God's perfect qualities should bring us great peace and confidence.

God is also just. This means he will always do the right thing. He is always fair. Deuteronomy 32:4 says all his ways are justice. He will never mistreat us, never play favorites, and always punish wrongdoing in his time. Thank God for his justice. There are many more attributes about God such as loving, compassionate, peaceful, gracious, kind, truthful, all-powerful, all-knowing, and ever-present. He is also our Father. What a relationship we can have with God! The more you get to know him, the more you will love him.

Reflection:

1. How does knowing God's character help our relationship with him?

2. How have you seen God's goodness in your life?

3. What other qualities of God's character can you list or describe?

Notes:

Action Step:

LIGHT UP THE DARK
Grab a flashlight. Stand in the middle of the room in the dark and shine the flashlight on something in the room. How does God (light) protect us from things in the dark (sin)? What happens if we try to walk around in the dark without the flashlight? Discuss what a flashlight does to the dark (makes it disappear, shows things we could trip over, etc.). How is God our light?

Our Prayer For You:

Jesus, thank you for being perfect in every way. God, thank you for being a loving and good Father. The more we discover your character, the more we love you. As we read your Word, help us see your clearer. Reveal yourself more and more in our lives. Help us see how good, holy, and just you are. In Jesus' name we pray, Amen.

GOD'S LOVE

Bible Verse:

"We love because he first loved us."   -1 John 4:19

Something to Think About:

Have you ever loved something or someone? Love is one of the greatest words you could ever experience. We give and receive love. It is the act of showing God's love to others. God loved us first (1 John 4:19). It is great to say we love God, but we only know real love because of his love. In fact, God is love (1 John 4:8, 16). We use the world love loosely these days. We say, "I love tacos" and "I love God". I think those are two very different statements, and I'm not sure you can really love tacos in the same way you love God. God doesn't just love us, he is love. It's not just an action he performs, but his true nature. When he gives love, it is pure and perfect. We can trust his love.

The greatest expression of God's love was through Jesus' death on the cross for our sin. 1 John 4:10 says he loved us and sent Jesus to pay for our sin. Romans 5:8 is the clearest verse about God's love through Jesus. It says, "God demonstrated his love for us in this: While we were sinners, Christ died for us." Love always shows itself to be true. We thank God for loving us so much that he sent Jesus to be our Savior.

Truth to Treasure:
God doesn't just love us, he is love.

Because God loves us and we have experienced how he has changed our lives, we should love others. We should "love God with all of our heart, soul, mind, and strength, and love our neighbor as ourselves" (Mark 12:30-31). As God shows more and more of his love to us, we should give that love away through serving, compassion, and mercy in very practical and meaningful ways. God loves you. We love Him. We must love others with His love.

Reflection:

1. What other Scriptures do you know about God's love?

2. How do you need God's love today?

3. How can you show God's love to someone else in your life?

Notes:

Action Step:

GIVE US CLEAN HEARTS
This activity will take a little preparation. Buy a red craft foam sheet. Cut out 7-9" hearts. With WASHABLE markers, have kids write sins on the hearts. Use soapy water to erase the sins from the hearts.
TEST FIRST for best results.
What are some Scriptures you can say while washing? How does God washing away or sins show his love?

Our Prayer For You:

Jesus, thank you for loving us and giving your life on the cross for our sins. You are love. As we experience your love, help us give your love away to others. As we do, may we tell others about you in hopes they will know your saving love as well. Thank you for loving us first. In Jesus' name we pray, Amen.

AVOID SIN

Bible Verse:

"Do not set foot on the path of the wicked or walk in the way of evildoers. Avoid it, do not travel on it; turn from it and go on your way."
-Proverbs 4:14-15

Something to Think About:

Have you ever broken a rule? What about disobeyed your parents? Sin is defined as disobeying God's Word and rebelling against God. Sin separates us from God (Isaiah 59:2). 1 John 3:4 says, "Sin is lawlessness". Sin is a disregard for God's law or Word. When we ignore or disobey God's Word, we sin. Sin can be doing something wrong and not doing something right. For instance, God's Word says, "Don't steal" (Exodus 20:15). We sin when we steal. God's Word also says, "Give thanks at all times" (1 Thessalonians 5:18). We sin when we don't give thanks.

Sin begins in our hearts. It is often done in our thoughts before it becomes an action. The best way to avoid sin is to hide God's Word in our hearts. Psalm 119:11 says, "I have hidden God's Word in my heart that I might not sin against God." Another way to avoid sin is being careful who we hang around. 1 Corinthians 15:33 says, "Bad company corrupts good habits."

Truth to Treasure:
The best way to avoid sin is to hide God's Word in our hearts.

The opposite is also true – good company encourages good habits. We must choose friends who will help us avoid sin.

God helps us avoid sin. When we are tempted to sin, God always gives us a way out. He builds in an escape hatch into every situation. 1 Corinthians 10:13 says God is faithful and gives us a way out when we are tempted. He will give us the strength to obey Him and run from sin. When all else fails, run from sin and to God. Whatever you do, follow James 4:7. It says, "Submit to God. Resist the devil, and he will flee."

Reflection:

1. What are some ways we can avoid sin?

2. Why is sin bad?

3. Do you struggle with any sins?

Notes:

Action Step:

THE DOMINO EFFECT OF SIN
Find a set of dominoes and ask your kids to stack them in a line one by one. Ultimately, one will fall and knock the other ones down. Discuss how one sin can lead to another. Talk about how our sins can affect others. Remind them that sooner or later, our sins will destroy things in our lives.

Our Prayer For You:

Jesus, help me to avoid sin. I know I must hide your Word in my heart by reading, memorizing, and meditating on it. Help me hang around people who love you and hate sin. Help me say no to sin when I am tempted. Thank you for giving me a way out to be free from sinning. In Jesus' name we pray, Amen.

AVOID FOOLISHNESS

Bible Verse:

"The fool says in his heart, 'There is no God'".
-Psalm 14:1

Something to Think About:

The Bible tells us there are two types of people – foolish and wise. A foolish person is someone who ignores and disobeys God's Word. The book of Proverbs describes a foolish person. They hate knowledge, ignore advice, enjoy wickedness, disobey their parents, speak evil things, often get angry, stir up trouble, and deceive others. A foolish person also says there is no God (Psalm 14:1)! Foolish people refuse to learn from their past mistakes, are often prideful, and hate to take advice from others. Foolishness has less to do with a person's intelligence and more to do with their character and attitude.

What does a wise person look like? First, a wise person learns and applies God's Word to their lives. In the parable of the Wise and Foolish Builder in Matthew 7:24-27, Jesus said, "Everyone who hears these words of mine and puts them into practice is like a wise man who built his house on the rock." A wise person also "walks with the wise" (Proverbs 13:20). You need wise friends who follow Jesus. A wise person also listens to advice from wise people. Proverbs 12:15 says, "The way of a fool is right in his own eyes, but a wise man is he who listens to counsel."

Truth to Treasure:
All wisdom comes from God.

A wise person also asks God for wisdom. James 1:5 says if we lack wisdom, we should ask God and he will give it to us. Ask God to help you grow in wisdom. He will! All wisdom comes from God and he will help us all stay far away from foolishness.

Reflection:

1. What's are the differences between wisdom and foolishness?

2. What's the most important way to avoid foolishness and gain wisdom?

3. How important are friends when it comes to wisdom and foolishness?

Notes:

Action Step:

WISE OR FOOLISH?
Have your child stand across the room from you. When you make a statement, they must step forward if they think it's wise or stay still if foolish. When they reach you, hug and pray with them about wisdom. Examples: pray for someone, hit someone back, give to the poor, steal something you want, say thank you, call someone a bad name, etc.

Our Prayer For You:

Jesus, help us to avoid foolishness. We want humble and teachable hearts. We ask you to give us our wisdom. Help us walk with the wise. We want to learn and practice your Word. We want to build my life on you the Solid Rock. In Jesus' name we pray, Amen.

AVOID LAZINESS

Bible Verse:

"How long will you lie there, you sluggard? When will you get up from your sleep?"

-Proverbs 6:9

Something to Think About:

Have you ever had a "lazy day"? This usually an expression to describe a day of rest or relaxation after a busy time. There's nothing wrong with slowing down and taking time off. This is very different than being a lazy person. When the Bible talks about laziness, it is never in a good way. Laziness is the avoidance of work. God created us to work. In Genesis 2:15, God placed Adam in the garden to work and take care of it. He told them to "be fruitful and multiply" (Genesis 1:28). Colossians 3:23 tell us whatever we do, work at it with all your heart, as working for the Lord. This can be our work or homework from school, cleaning our room, and doing our chores. When we constantly put off the work we must do or try to do as little of it as possible, we are being lazy.

Truth to Treasure:
God created us to work and not be lazy.

In the parable of the bags of gold in Matthew 25:14-29, Jesus tells about three servants who are entrusted with their boss' money. Each received different amounts (5, 2, and 1 bag). The one with five put it to work and doubled it – so did the one with two. The one with one bag did nothing. When the master returned, he called the first two "good and faithful servants" and the last one "wicked and lazy". God expects us to work with all he has entrusted us. We should want to be good and faithful servants of God with our time, money, work, and resources.

Be a hard worker. Lazy people want good things, but don't want to work for them. Work hard at school, hobbies, jobs, relationships, and growing in Jesus. Be disciplined and determined to work hard at all you do.

Reflection:

1. What's the difference between laziness and rest?

2. What's are some results of laziness? What are some results of hard work?

3. In what areas of life do you tend to be lazy?

Notes:

Action Step:

EXCUSES, EXCUSES
Find a chore that needs to be completed (in your child's room is best). Say, "We need to do this chore. What are some lazy even crazy excuses to why we can't be responsible?" Example: I can't pick up my dirty clothes because the stink might melt my arm off. That's a crazy answer! Discuss why God wants us to be responsible with what he has given us.

Our Prayer For You:

Jesus, help us not be lazy. We want to be good and faithful servants in all you have called us to do in life. Help us not avoid or put off work but do it with all our heart, soul, mind, and strength. Discipline us to grow in what you've entrusted us so we can use our work as worship for you. In Jesus' name we pray, Amen.

AVOID PRIDE

Bible Verse:

"Pride goes before destruction, a haughty spirit before a fall."
                                                            -Proverbs 16:18

Something to Think About:

What is pride? There's a "good" pride, like being proud of your family or friends for accomplishing something. Paul had this kind of pride in the Corinthians when he said, "I have great pride in you…I am overflowing with joy" (2 Corinthians 7:4). This can be when they win an award or even excel in something at school. This isn't the kind of pride the Bible calls bad. That kind of pride is selfish, arrogant, and doesn't want God's teaching or help. Proverbs 16:18 says is destructive and will result in falling away from God.

The opposite of pride is humility. When you are humble, you think of others first, ask for help, are teachable, and desire to serve God. Proud people take all the credit for themselves and never thank God or others for helping them. Matthew 5:3 says, "Blessed are the poor in spirit for theirs is the Kingdom of Heaven." "Poor in spirit" means you need God because you know you are weak and imperfect. A humble person knows anything they accomplish is because God gave them the ability, strength, and wisdom to do it. They know God deserves all the glory for everything they do.

Truth to Treasure: **The opposite of pride is humility.**

Pride takes all the credit. Humility gives God all the credit. Pride promotes self. Humility promotes God and others. Pride wants praise. Humility gives praise. Pride compares. Humility is content. Pride condemns. Humility encourages. Stay away from pride in all its forms. Practice humility in everything you do, and you'll be like Jesus (Philippians 2:6-11).

Reflection:

1. What's the difference between pride and humility?

2. What are some signs you are being prideful?

3. Are there areas of your life you try to do without the help of God and others?

Notes:

Action Step:

PICTURE THE PARABLE
Read the parable of the Tax Collector and the Pharisee in Luke 18:10-14. Draw a picture of each of person in the story. Describe each one's posture, words, and attitude. Write words on the picture to describe both people. Talk about how our actions, words, and attitudes display whether we are humble or prideful.

Our Prayer For You:

Jesus, help us not be prideful but humble. You took on the nature of a servant when you went to the cross for our sins. Thank you for showing us how to live in humility. We don't want to be selfish, arrogant, or unteachable. Remind us we are totally dependent on you for everything. In Jesus' name we pray, Amen.

AVOID GOSSIP

Bible Verse:

"A perverse person stirs up conflict, and a gossip separates close friends."
-Proverbs 16:28

Something to Think About:

Gossip is a terrible form of communication – it is sharing true or false information with someone that doesn't need to know it and can't do anything to help. Gossip is destructive to relationships because it is usually done behind someone's back in a secret way. Sometimes gossip pretends to be sincere concern, like "pray for them because …", and then never gets around to praying. Gossip hurts the people being talked about and the people doing the talking.

Proverbs 16:28 says gossip will separate close friends. If someone is your friend, you shouldn't talk about them behind their back or spread information that could be hurtful or untrue. Friends talk face to face with friends. If you don't know if something is true, you shouldn't share it with others. Instead, you should say something like, "I'm not sure that's accurate, let's go talk to them about it." Loving your friends means you help stop others from potentially gossiping and harming them. Friends stop gossip!

Truth to Treasure:

Gossips stop friendships.

The Bible has something to say about people who love to gossip. Proverbs 20:19 says don't hang around those who go around gossiping. It calls them troublemakers (Proverbs 16:28) and untrustworthy (Proverbs 11:13). If you don't want to be known that way, don't gossip. Instead, "speak the truth in love" (Ephesians 4:15) to your friends. "Quarrels stop when gossip stops" (Proverbs 26:20).

Reflection:

1. What's wrong with gossip?

2. Have you ever been guilty of gossiping?

3. How do you keep from gossiping?

Notes:

Action Step:

GOSSIP GLITTER

Grab a container of glitter and pour some in your child's hand. Tell your child they must pass the glitter to the next person (or place it all in a cup if they are the only person) without spilling it. No glitter can be on their hand, clothing, floor, table, etc. It's impossible! Discuss how glitter and gossip are similar (shiny, messy, stick around a long time, etc.).

Our Prayer For You:

Jesus, keep us from being known as gossips. We want to be people who speak the truth in all ways. When we hear information about a friend, help us uphold truth and protect their reputation. Let us talk with our friends face to face in love when we have concerns. In Jesus' name we pray, Amen.

AVOID SELFISHNESS

Bible Verse:

"Don't look to your own interests but each of you to the interests of the others."
-Philippians 2:4

Something to Think About:

Selfishness is a problem for everyone. We are selfish by nature. We often want what we want when we want it. All too often, we spend too much time thinking about ourselves. When we are selfish, we are only caring about our desires and needs. Selfishness causes us to be preoccupied with our wants and oblivious to the needs of others. How do we keep from being selfish people?

The opposite of selfishness is generosity. Qualities such as compassion, kindness, and love keep us from being selfish. The Apostle Paul told the Philippian Christians to not only look out for their own interests but also to the interests of others. We all have things we must personally think about and do, but we must think about others as well. Only thinking about yourself is what selfishness is! Paul goes on to say Christ's humility included "emptying" or not thinking about himself. Jesus said his followers must forget about themselves and take up their cross (Luke 9:23).

Truth to Treasure:
Selfishness leads to many other sins.

One way to combat selfishness is to practice generosity. Instead of asking "What is this going to cost me?", ask "How can I help out of what God has given me?". Selfishness causes many other sinful practices. James 3:16 says, "Where you have selfishness and envy, you find disorder and every evil practice." If we see someone in need, we should show them the love of God through helping them (1 John 3:17). In all you do, be generous, kind, helpful, and loving.

Reflection:

1. In what ways are we often selfish? Why?

2. What keeps us from being selfish?

3. In what ways was Jesus generous?

Notes:

Action Step:
SELFISH SERVINGS
During a regular meal, arrange all the food on the table only in front of you. Instead of using your plate, say, "I'm going to just eat from the containers since all this is for me". Place your arms around the food and begin to eat. What are everyone's reactions? Discuss how selfishness affects others and how it makes everyone feel. How is sharing better?

Our Prayer For You:
Jesus, we do not want anything to do with selfishness. Help us to be like you: loving, giving, sacrificial, and a blessing to others. Help us practice generosity and kindness with everyone we meet. When we are able to help others, show us practical ways to display your love to them. In Jesus' name we pray, Amen.

GUARD YOUR HEART

Bible Verse:

"Above all else, guard your heart, for everything you do flows from it."
-Proverbs 4:23

Something To Think About:

A security guard's job is to protect people and places from intruders or damage. They do their best to see that no harm comes to those around them. We need to be security guards over our hearts. Our hearts can be damaged by sin and so many destructive things. The devil wants to break in and "steal, kill, and destroy" from our lives (John 10:10). How do we guard our hearts? Why are they so important?

Proverbs 4:23 says to guard our hearts "above all else". That means the heart is the most important and most valuable thing we have. The Scripture continues, "everything you do flows from it". The writer of this proverb isn't warning us about protecting our hearts from being hurt. He is cautioning us against allowing sin and evil in our lives because they can destroy every part of our lives. In the Bible, the heart refers to a person's thoughts, emotions, desires, and understanding. It is the inner us that controls the outer us.

Truth To Treasure:
We must guard our hearts from sin.

To guard against sin and evil, we must agree with God about what they are. His Word describes sin and its destructive nature so well. We must read and obey God's Word, repent of sin, seek God's righteousness, and protect what we think about. We must desire to be holy as God is holy (1 Peter 1:16). We must allow the Holy Spirit to lead us to truth and convict us of sin. One Bible translation calls our hearts the "wellspring" of life. Polluted waters can cause disease and death. We must allow God's Word to wash our hearts and make them pure (Ephesians 5:26).

Reflection:

1. How important are our hearts (thoughts, emotions, desires, understanding)?

2. How do we guard our hearts from sin?

3. Is there an area of your heart that's been polluted with sin?

Notes:

HEART TAG *Action Step:*
Cut out a heart shape for every person playing and tape it to your back. The object of the game is to take the other person's heart. Play with as many people as possible. Guard your paper heart without hitting or hurting others. The person with the most hearts wins. Discuss what it means to guard your heart from sinful things (crude videos, unkind people, untrue thoughts, etc.).

Our Prayer For You:

Jesus, thank you for saving us. We desire to have pure hearts and clean hands (Psalm 24:3). We do not want sin to pollute our thoughts, attitudes, emotions, actions, desires, or understanding. Help us guard our hearts by the protection of your Word and Spirit. In Jesus' name we pray, Amen.

GUARD YOUR MIND

Bible Verse:

"Who has known the mind of the Lord so as to instruct him? But we have the mind of Christ."

-1 Corinthians 2:16

Something to Think About:

What do you think about most often? Sometimes, our thoughts can run wild. We can imagine things that aren't true and potentially harmful to our lives. Most of the time, our actions and words start in our thoughts. Belief controls behavior. What controls your mind controls you. There is a battle for your thoughts and God wants you to win, but it won't happen without a spiritual fight.

Having the mind of Christ is our goal. When Paul said, "We have the mind of Christ" in 1 Corinthians 2:16, he was saying our minds should match that of Jesus. We should think, reason, and respond from the truth of Christ and His Word. He even asks, "who instructs the Lord?" He knows best! There is a battle for our thoughts. Paul also wrote, "For though we live in the world, we do not wage war as the world does. The weapons we fight with are not the weapons of the world. On the contrary, they have divine power to demolish strongholds. We demolish arguments and every pretension that sets itself up against the knowledge of God, and we take captive every thought to make it obedient to Christ" (2 Corinthians 10:3-5). The weapons God gives us to fight with are the Word, prayer, faith, righteousness, God's truth, the gospel, and more from Ephesians 6:13-18.

Truth to Treasure:
What controls your mind controls you.

We protect our minds by carefully selecting what we put in them: what we read, listen to, where we go. This includes tv, music, conversations, etc. May our thoughts give glory and honor to Jesus.

Reflection:

1. Why is our thought life so important in our walk with Jesus?

2. How do we guard our minds from sinful thoughts?

3. Is there an area of your thought life that you need prayer for?

Notes:

A MILKY MIND *Action Step:*
Get a clear glass of milk, a pitcher of water, and a pan. The milk represents bad thoughts. The water the mind of Christ. Place the glass of milk in the pan. As you pour the water in the milk, let it overflow, and name some good thoughts we can have in Christ. Talk about how our mind becomes clearer (pure) when we pour more of Christ and His Word in it. Pour the water until it becomes clear.

Our Prayer For You:

Jesus, thank you for giving us the mind of Christ. Help us take thoughts captive and make them obey your truth. I want my thoughts to be your thoughts. Correct any wrong thinking, attitude, or belief in my life. Cleanse my mind and give me holy and pure thoughts. In Jesus' name we pray, Amen.

GUARD YOUR MOUTH

Bible Verse:

"Those who guard their lips preserve their lives, but those who speak rashly will come to ruin."

-Proverbs 13:3

Something to Think About:

Do you remember any words spoken to you that encouraged you? Maybe someone said they loved you or were proud of you. Do you remember any words that hurt you? Maybe someone called you a bad name or lied about you. Our words are powerful. They can either build others up or tear them down. As Solomon said in Proverbs 18:21, "Death and life are in the power of the tongue". We must be careful with our words. Careless words can crush our friends and discourage those closest to us. Careful words can give hope and encourage.

We must be intentional with the words we speak. We do this by thinking about what we say before we say it. We must ask, "Will this help or hurt? Would Jesus approve of the words I'm about to say?" In Ephesians 4:29, Paul tells us, "Don't let any unwholesome talk come out of your mouths, but only what is helpful for building others up according to their needs,

Truth to Treasure:
Our words have the power of life and death.

that it may benefit those who listen." Unwholesome talk could be sarcasm, gossip, lies, slander, or coarse joking. These do not please the Lord. Psalm 19:14 asks the Lord to make our words pleasing to Him and reminds us they come from our hearts just as Jesus said (Matthew 15:18).

James describes the tongue as a spark that can burn down an entire forest. We must learn to guard our mouths (Proverbs 13:3). The best way to do this is to put God's Word in our hearts and let him shape what comes out of our mouths.

Reflection:

1. Do your words heal or hurt?

2. Do you struggle with lying, slander, gossip, sarcasm, or coarse joking?

3. How do you guard what comes out of your mouth?

Notes:

Action Step:

BLESSING JAR
Find a clear jar or cup. Make a label that says "blessing jar" and tape it to the jar. This next week, every time you say something that is a blessing, nice, encouraging, etc. place a quarter (or whatever you want) in the jar. At the end of the week, discuss how you can use that money to bless someone else.

Our Prayer For You:

Jesus, your Word is life giving. As you change our hearts, our words will also change. We pray our words reflect your character and give you praise. If our words have hurt others, may we speak words of repentance and grace. Help us use our words to bless, encourage, and speak truth. In Jesus' name we pray, Amen.

GUARD YOUR EYES

Bible Verse:

"The eye is the lamp of the body. If your eyes are healthy, your whole body will be full of light. But if your eyes are unhealthy, your whole body will be full of darkness."   -Matthew 6:22-23

Something to Think About:

Thank God for the gift of sight! Our eyes allow us to see all God has wonderfully created and lead us to praise Him! Our eyes can also allow sinful things into our mind and heart. Jesus said our eyes are like windows to the soul. We must not allow the devil to have open access to our thoughts, emotions, words, and actions through looking at sinful things.

The psalmist said, "I will set no wicked thing before my eyes" (Psalm 101:3). This includes what we watch on tv, the internet, and read. What we allow into our lives through our eyes can either grow us spiritually stronger in the Lord or cause us to sin and hurt our relationship with God. The psalmist gives us a practical step in keeping sinful things out of our sight. He says don't put them in front of you! This means, don't choose to look at them and if they do get in your sight, do whatever it takes to remove them.

Truth to Treasure: *Our eyes are windows to our souls.*

One of the best things to look at is God's Word. We should think about it all the time. Joshua 1:8 says to meditate on it day and night. What we look at will affect every other part of us. God's Word will shape us to look like Him in all ways. Just like you would put on sunglasses to protect your eyes, you and I must place spiritual filters on our eyes. If we want to keep our hearts and minds pure, we must remember it starts with our eyes. Hebrews 12:2 says we "fix our eyes on Jesus, the author and perfector of our faith". Keep your eyes on Jesus and keep them away from anything not for Jesus.

Reflection:

1. Why is it important to guard our eyes from sinful things?

2. What sins can begin with a wrong look?

3. What are some Bible verses to help keep our eyes focused on the Lord?

Notes:

Action Step:

SPIRITUAL BLINDNESS
Grab a blindfold (handkerchief, scarf, towel, etc.). Have one person place it over their eyes. Have another person go across the room and give directions to the blindfolded person to come to them. Discuss how difficult it is when you cannot see and how important our eyes are for seeing spiritually.

Our Prayer For You:

Jesus, keep our eyes from worthless and sinful things. Help us to look to you the author and perfector of our faith. We want to look at all of your wonderful creation and praise you. Thank you for giving us your Word to read and influence every area of our lives. Help us see your beauty. In Jesus' name we pray, Amen.

GUARD YOUR EMOTIONS

Bible Verse:

"Do not be anxious about anything, but in every situation, pray…"
-Philippians 4:6

Something to Think About:

Our emotions can often be like a roller coaster – up and down, twisted, even downright scary! Emotions are not bad, but they can become out of control. Our emotions express everything from joy to sadness. God's Word helps us guard our emotions. Philippians 4:6-7 says, *"Do not be anxious about anything, but in every situation, by prayer and petition, with thanksgiving, present your requests to God. And the peace of God, which transcends all understanding, will guard your hearts and your minds in Christ Jesus."*

When we are anxious, we should pray. We should also remember to thank God for who He is and what He has done and promised in His Word. This will build our trust in Him and quiet our raging emotions. Prayer and thanks leads to peace and His presence! Refocusing our minds to think about Him and His Word are sure ways to guard, renew, and settle our emotions.

Truth to Treasure:
The peace and presence of God will settle our emotions.

What should we think about instead when our emotions seem out of control? Philippians 4:8 continues, *"Whatever is true, whatever is noble, whatever is right, whatever is pure, whatever is lovely, whatever is admirable–if anything is excellent or praiseworthy–think about such things."* Our emotions are connected to our thoughts. For our emotions to be healthy, they must be managed by our thoughts. Proverbs 14:30 in the MSG says, *"A sound mind makes for a robust body, but runaway emotions corrode the bones."* Don't let your emotions run away from you and hurt the rest of you. Let God heal and control them.

Reflection:

1. What is your favorite emotion? What is your least favorite emotion?

2. How do we settle our emotions when they become out of control?

3. What emotion do you struggle with the most?

Notes:

Action Step:

LIST OF EMOTIONS
Write down your favorite emotion. List the reasons it is your favorite. Write down your least favorite emotion. List the reasons it is your least favorite. Discuss how God can work in both our favorite and least favorite emotions.

Our Prayer For You:

Jesus, thank you helping us calm our emotions. We desire your peace and presence. When our emotions become out of control, help us think about you and your word and ways. Help us use prayer and thanksgiving as a means to remember you who brings peace and comfort. In Jesus' name we pray, Amen.

GUARD YOUR TIME

Bible Verse:

"Make the most of every opportunity, because the days are evil."
-Ephesians 5:16

Something to Think About:

How do you spend your time? We say "spend" because, like money, we only have so much time. We can either invest our time wisely or waste it foolishly. Think about yesterday? How did you spend your day? Did you take time to talk to God through prayer? Did you read your Bible and learn about God? Did you use your time to be kind, generous, and loving toward someone else? There are many things we can do with our time, but God wants us to use it well for His praise.

What wastes your time? Silly Tik Tok or YouTube videos? Video games? One way to guard our time is to remember to "make the most of opportunity" like Ephesians 5:16 says. The verse continues, "because the days are evil". This means we should use our time to do things that please God, not for things that are evil. When you begin your day spending time with God, it sets the tone for the rest of the day on how you will use your time. When you read

Truth to Treasure:
We must spend our time wisely, not waste it foolishly.

a Bible verse on being loving or serving someone else, you should spend your time looking for ways to do that. When you pray for God to keep you from sin, you will be more focused on living holy that day instead of giving into temptation.

The first part of the Great Commandment (Matthew 22:36-40) says, "Love God with all your heart, soul, mind, and strength." This is really everything you do with your time! Write down how you will spend your time with God in each of these areas today. Don't waste your time on foolish things. Guard your time with God and grow in Him all day long.

Reflection:

1. What do you spend most of your "free time" doing?

2. What's your favorite thing to do with your time?

3. Do you have any time wasters?

Notes:

Action Step:
IT'S TIME TO GROW
Grab a sheet of paper and write down each hour you are awake a whole day (7am, 8am, 9am, etc.). Write down what you do most days during that time. Now, write down how you could make that time more productive for the Lord.
Example: 7am - breakfast - pray
Noon - lunch - eat with a friend
8pm - bedtime - read Scripture

Our Prayer For You:

Jesus, thank you helping us spend our time wisely, not foolishly. We desire to invest our lives one day at a time, one hour at a time, growing in You and doing your will. Help us keep from doing things that waste the precious time you've given us. May our time be used in worship to you. In Jesus' name we pray, Amen.

GUARD YOUR TALENTS

Bible Verse:

"Each of you should use whatever gift you have received to serve others, as faithful stewards of God's grace in its various forms."
-1 Peter 4:10

Something to Think About:

Everyone wants to be good at something. There are so many talent-based reality TV shows that promote being the best at something whether it's singing, dancing, cooking, or something else. The problem with the approach of these shows is the talents are about the person and not the Giver of the talents. God created and gifted us with special talents to use for His purposes. When we are good at or grow in a special ability or talent, the tendency of our flesh is to use it to promote ourselves and not God. God gives us spiritual gifts, talents, and abilities not to highlight us but him. Therefore, we must guard our talents and use them to praise him and build his Kingdom.

According to 1 Peter 4:10, there are "various forms" of gifts God has graciously given us. We must use them to serve others in Jesus' name. Romans 12 and 1 Corinthians 12 tell us we have gifts to serve as the "body of Christ" with many different parts.

Truth to Treasure:
God gave us talents to use for His purposes.

For example, some have the gift of generosity and others have the gift of service. While every follower of Jesus should be generous and serve, extra grace is given to some to use these gifts in extraordinary ways for God's glory to build up His Church.

If we ever use our abilities and gifts to promote ourselves, we are using them wrong. To guard our talents, we just put them to work for God in what He has prepared for us to do in his will (Romans 10:9-10). Thank God for his gifts and ask him to help you use them for his glory.

Reflection:

1. What talents do you have that can be used for the Lord?

2. How are you using your talents for Jesus?

3. What keeps you from using your talents for the Lord?

Notes:

Action Step:

YOU'VE GOT TALENT
Identify one talent you have. Now, think about it. How could you use it at your church? School? Family? Neighborhood?

Write a couple ideas on how to use this talent in the areas above and ask God to help you do that this week.

Our Prayer For You:

Jesus, thank you for giving us gifts, talents, and abilities to use to love you and serve others. Help us use them in a humble way that points others to you. If we ever become proud and use them to highlight ourselves, remind us of your will and purposes. In Jesus' name we pray, Amen.

FEAR

Bible Verse:

"The Lord is my light and my salvation – whom shall I fear?
The Lord is the stronghold of my life – of whom shall I be afraid?"

-Psalm 27:1

Something to Think About:

Everyone is afraid of something. Whether it's spiders or heights, fear has paralyzed and intimidated us before in life. The Bible says fear has torment, but perfect love casts out fear (1 John 4:18). What are you afraid of? President Benjamin Harrison was so fearful when electricity was first introduced in the White House that he would not touch any of the light switches! If the lights were on at bed time, he slept with them on!

Maybe you're scared of the future. The "what if" questions are endless. Jesus said do not worry about tomorrow (Matthew 6:34). Maybe it's your past. We've all messed up and have things we regret. The Bible says in Christ we are new creations – the old has past and the new has come (2 Corinthians 5:17). Maybe you're scared of what you are going through right now. Second Corinthians 4:7-18 NLT says, "For our present troubles are small and won't last very long. Yet they produce for us a glory that vastly outweighs them and will last forever!"

Truth to Treasure:

God's perfect love casts out fear.

There is no shame in admitting our fears. That's when you begin to ask God for help. That's when you start depending on God and believing He can help you with anything. Paul told Timothy, "God hasn't given us a spirit of fear, but of power, love, and a sound mind" (2 Timothy 1:7). Giving your fear over to God doesn't mean you will never be afraid again. It means you believe God is with you every step of the way to comfort, strengthen, guide, and protect.

Reflection:

1. What are you afraid of?

2. How do we overcome fear?

3. Do you know any more Bible verses about fear?
(There are at least 365 – one for every day of the year!)

Notes:

FACE YOUR FEARS Action Step:

Fill a glass 3/4 of the way with water. Say: "This water represents our fears." Take a Styrofoam plate with the word "faith" written on it and place over cup. Say: "We must give our fears over to Jesus through faith". Hold your hand on the plate and turn the cup upside down. It should not spill (practice). We give our fears in faith to Jesus. Now, remove the cup over a sink and dump all your fears out.

Our Prayer For You:

Jesus, thank you for helping us overcome all our fears. Through faith, we admit our fears and give them to you. We believe you will help us in every situation in life, especially when it gets scary. We choose to trust in you for protection, strength, wisdom, comfort, and guidance. In Jesus' name we pray, Amen.

LONELINESS

Bible Verse:

"And they will name him Immanuel, meaning God with us."
                                            -Matthew 1:23

Something to Think About:

Being alone and being lonely are two different things. We've all be alone at times without anyone else around, but the feelings of loneliness are more than the temporary lack of someone's presence. The feelings of loneliness can be present in a room full of people. When you don't believe you have any friends or anyone on your side, it can leave you depressed and hopeless. On at least one occasion, David expressed his loneliness to God. He said, "Turn to me and be gracious to me, for I am lonely and afflicted. Relieve the troubles of my heart and free me from my anguish" (Psalm 25:16-17). It is good to know that when we feel lonely, we can turn to Jesus and ask Him for help.

One of the reasons we can turn to Jesus is He is Immanuel, which means "God with us" (Matthew 1:23). Psalm 46:1 tells us "God is our refuge and strength, an ever-present help in time of need." This should bring us great comfort that God is always with us to bring strength and help. God said, "Never will I leave you, never will I forsake you" (Hebrews 13:5). Loneliness is something we all face from time to time. Thankfully, God is always with us. We can depend on Him!

Truth to Treasure:
One of Jesus' names is Immanuel, "God with us".

Our church family is also a gift to help us when loneliness attacks. God designed church to be a community and family of faith. He "sets the lonely in families" (Psalm 68:6). Church is our brothers and sisters in the faith. We pray for, encourage, love, and serve one another as a church family. When you are feeling lonely, pray to God and reach out to someone in your church for help and prayer.

Reflection:

1. What makes you feel lonely?

2. How do you deal with lonely feelings?

3. How can you experience more of God's presence and your church families' support in times of loneliness?

Notes:

TEAM WORK *Action Step:*

Grab a deck of cards. Blindfold your child and give them 30 seconds to build a house of cards with four sides and a roof on their own. Next, try again, but this time help them by coaching them the entire minute. Next, coach them, but on the first step, remove their blindfold and help them build it. Talk about which was hardest and easiest. Discuss the importance of others in our lives.

Our Prayer For You:

Jesus, thank you for helping us in times of loneliness. Help us remember you are ever present. As you said in Matthew 28:20, "I am with you always". Thank your presence, strength, help, and comfort. May we remember the importance of community in our church family. In Jesus' name we pray, Amen.

DISAPPOINTMENT

Bible Verse:

"And we know that in all things God works for the good of those who love him, who have been called according to his purpose."
                                                            -Romans 8:28

Something to Think About:

We all face disappointment. Sometimes things don't go as you hoped they would. When we are disappointed, we are hurt in some way because a different result has happened that we didn't expect. When we are hurt, we can lose hope. A Scripture God uses to help remind us He's in control and can be trusted when things do go our way is Romans 8:28. It says God is at work in every situation doing good in those who love Him and called to His purpose. God is at work even when we are disappointed. He even uses less than ideal situations to display His beauty. God doesn't just work in perfect scenarios. He's always at work. Trusting God in the imperfect and unexpected is important because He desires to use every situation to display His beauty and power.

Truth to Treasure:
Disappointment can rob the new God wants to do.

What causes disappointment in your life? Do you set unrealistic goals? Do you have an unhealthy view of how everything should go? Have people let you down? Whatever reason disappointment happens, we can find encouragement from the Lord. Psalm 30:5 says, "Weeping may last for a night, but joy comes in the morning." That means God can bring joy to your life even if we experience loss or when what we hope for doesn't come true. Those things attempt to keep us from experiencing and believing God has good plans for us. We can either hold on to disappointment or allow God to give us a fresh perspective. He is good no matter what. When we choose to let go of disappointments, we can embrace the new God is doing. In Isaiah 43:9, God says, "Behold, I am doing something new. Can you perceive it?" If we hold on to disappointment, we will miss seeing and experience everything God wants to do.

Reflection:

1. Are you struggling with disappointment?

2. What causes you to get stuck in disappointment?

3. What Bible characters could have allowed disappointment to ruin all God wanted to do in their lives?

Notes:

LIMBO — *Action Step:*

Grab a stick and play limbo. As you dodge the stick, talk about how we must not allow disappointment to get us off track. At some point, the limbo stick (disappointment) will stop us. Will you give up, or will you play again? How can you keep going even when disappointment comes? Talk about what the word "limbo" means (uncertainty, waiting without hope) and how to overcome it.

Our Prayer For You:

Jesus, when we are disappointed, we chose to allow you to encourage us and get us back on track. We ask you to change our perspective and help us see the new you want to do. We believe you can make all things work for our good. We love you and thank you for calling us to love and serve you. In Jesus' name we pray, Amen.

GRIEF

Bible Verse:

"Blessed are those who mourn, for they will be comforted."
              -Matthew 5:4

Something to Think About:

We have all lost things. Some things we lose are easily replaced. Some things we lose are not. It's one thing to lose a jacket and another to lose your pet. The jacket is easily replaced, but the puppy has emotional connections and is a living being. Anytime we lose something close to us, there will be hurt to some degree. If you lose a friend because they move or because you got in a fight, there are many feelings and emotions to work through. If someone close to you dies, deep hurt and loss are certain, and grief can affect you for years or the rest of your life. How do you walk through loss in a healthy way that brings comfort, peace, and healing?

Grief is hard because certain joys are damaged or gone. It feels as if in those moments you just cannot go on and will forever be hurt and affected beyond repair. One thing we must remember is Jesus is familiar with our grief. Isaiah 53:3 says, "He was despised and rejected by men, a man of sorrows and acquainted with grief." Jesus understands loss as the Bible tells us he grieved when John the Baptist (his cousin) and Lazarus (his friend) died. John 11:33 tell us "When Jesus saw Mary weeping...he (Jesus) was deeply moved in his Spirit and troubled." Then, he wept with her (John 11:35). We have a God who understands grief and grieves with us in our time of loss and sadness.

Truth to Treasure: **Jesus understands and is our hope in our grief.**

One Scripture to keep in mind is 1 Thessalonians 4:13, which says, "Do not grieve like the rest of mankind, who have no hope." Jesus is our hope when we grieve. He will comfort and help us in our grief and is our hope over death in eternity.

Reflection:

1. Have you ever experienced loss and grief?

2. What are your reactions, emotion, and feelings when you experience loss and grief?

3. How does Jesus help us when we grieve?

Notes:

EXPRESSING GRIEF *Action Step:*
If (or when) your child is experiencing grief, one way they can express and process it if they cannot do it verbally is through art. Perhaps they can draw what they are feeling or thinking. That brings moments to pray, discuss Scripture, listen, and encourage. Often kids can be overlooked in times of loss. Seek out a professional and biblical counselor in these times to help your child.

Our Prayer For You:

Jesus, when we experience loss we are thankful you also experienced it and can help us. You understand what we feel and can comfort and encourage us with your hope and peace. Help us look to you in times of sorrow and heal our wounds when we are hurt. We love and trust you. In Jesus' name we pray, Amen.

UNCERTAINTY

Bible Verse:

"Trust in him at all times, you people; pour out your hearts to him, for God is our refuge."

-Psalm 62:8

Something to Think About:

Life can be unclear and unpredictable at times. It's unavoidable. We face questions about our future, health, finances, relationships, and many other things we don't have immediate answers for. This can cause fear and even panic, but it doesn't have to. Trusting God is the antidote to uncertainty. You may think having an immediate clear answer is the antidote, but that's not always something we receive. Clarity may seem like the best answer to uncertainty, but actually trust in God is what we need. We must depend on God in every moment of our lives and allow Him to direct our steps.

Psalm 62:8 says, "Trust in him at all times." When we don't know the answer to something in life, when we are troubled about our next step, or if we are fearful of what may happen in our future, we must surrender our fear, worry, and anxiety to God. Knowing the next step doesn't always take our fears away – but God can even if we don't know the next step. Faith is being sure of what we do not see (Hebrews 11:6). Our hope and our trust must be in God. He will give us answers, insight, and next steps in his way and time. We can trust him because of his faithfulness and goodness.

Truth to Treasure:
The antidote for uncertainty is trust in God.

When you are overwhelmed with uncertainty, don't allow panic and worry to overcome you. One way to combat panic is praise. Another way to overcome uncertainty is prayer and reading Scripture. It's in those times that we must be reminded of God's character, provision, and protection.

Reflection:

1. What are you uncertain about?

2. What feelings, emotions, thoughts, or actions does uncertainty cause in you?

3. How does Jesus help our uncertainty?

Notes:

Action Step:

GUESSING GAME
Find a picture of an animal, person, thing, etc. (it really doesn't matter). Cover the picture with several Post-It notes. Remove one Post-It note at a time and allow your child to guess what it is a picture of. Use this time to talk about uncertainty and guessing about things in life (the "what-ifs"). Talk about trust, hope, worry, peace, comfort, and other related things.

Our Prayer For You:

Jesus, when we are uncertain, we choose to trust in you. You have never failed us, and you never will. We need to be reminded of your faithfulness and goodness. When we are feeling anxious or afraid, we will pray and read the truth of your Word. Thank you for being trustworthy. In Jesus' name we pray, Amen.

HURT

Bible Verse:

"There will be no more death or mourning or crying or pain, for the old order of things has passed away."

-Revelation 21:4

Something to Think About:

All of us have experienced hurt of some kind. From a bike wreck that caused a knee scrape to an unfriendly word someone spoke to us, hurt can damage us in in many ways. Some hurt quickly decreases, like the scraped knee. Other hurt lingers, like the unkind words. We also experience hurt and pain when others we love experience hurt. One question that seems to come up when we are hurt is "Where is God in my pain?" Another is "Why did God allow my suffering?"

One day, in eternity, God will wipe away every tear and heal every hurt (Revelation 21:4). That should bring us great comfort. The Apostle Paul also said, "Our light, temporary nature of our suffering is producing for us an everlasting weight of glory, far beyond any comparison" (2 Corinthians 4:17). We know one day, heaven will be perfect and pain and suffering will stop. But, what about now?

Truth to Treasure:

God is with us in our suffering.

Forty-two of the Psalms are called Psalms of Lament (suffering). Psalm 34 says, "The Lord is close to the brokenhearted and saves those whose spirits are crushed" (18). Knowing God is present in our suffering and hurt brings great healing. God also puts people (the church) in our lives to help us in our times of suffering. Second Corinthians 1:4 reminds us, "We can comfort those in any trouble with the comfort we receive from God." God desires to help us heal from our hurts. One possible remedy for hurt is forgiving those who have hurt you (Colossians 3:13). Remember, Psalm 147:3 gives us great hope that, "He heals the brokenhearted and binds up their wounds."

Reflection:

1. Is there a lingering hurt in your life?

2. Is there any unforgiveness towards someone that's hurt you?

3. How can God use our hurts to cause spiritual growth and compassion for others?

Notes:

BAND-AID RELAY *Action Step:*
Grab a box of Band-Aids. Have your child stand against a wall with 5 Band-Aids on a chair. When you say go, have them grab one, run to you, unwrap it, and place it on you. They should run back to the remaining Band-Aids and repeat until none are left. Time this, then switch places with them and do the same to them. Talk about God's ability to heal our hurt during the game (even his miracles).

Our Prayer For You:

Jesus, thank you for healing our hurts. You understand and experienced suffering and pain. Help us bring our hurt to you, forgive others if necessary, and allow your Spirit and Word to minister healing in our lives. We desire to be whole and help others experience your healing power as well. In Jesus' name we pray, Amen.

WISDOM

Bible Verse:

"If any of you lacks wisdom, you should ask God, who gives generously to all without finding fault, and it will be given to you."
-James 1:5

Something to Think About:

One thing everyone needs to ask God for is wisdom. We all need it! Jesus' half-brother James said if we lack it, we should ask for it (James 1:5). Sometimes we ask for things from our parents, and we don't get them for good reasons. Maybe it's not in the budget, it's not necessarily needed, or we may be limited because of our behavior. The good news about wisdom is when we ask our Heavenly Father for it and we are guaranteed to get it! James continues by saying he, "gives generously to all without finding fault." God gives wisdom to us if we ask Him for it. We don't have it because we don't ask for it (James 4:2).

James gives us insight to know if we have obtained God's wisdom. James 3:17 says, "Wisdom that comes from heaven is first of all pure; then peace-loving, considerate, submissive, full of mercy and good fruit, impartial and sincere." When we ask God for wisdom, we should also ask ourselves and possibly others if we have increased peace, love, consideration for others, submission to God, mercy, good fruit, impartiality, and sincerity. If not, we may not be walking in the wisdom God has given. Asking God for wisdom is really us saying, "We need you God. We can't do anything without you."

Truth to Treasure:
God gives wisdom to us if we ask Him for it.

We need wisdom not just when we have a problem. We need God's wisdom to know how to serve others, love our families, how to walk in the Spirit, bring glory to God, and much more. We should keep asking God for it. He's the most trustworthy and loving guide for every part of our lives.

Reflection:

1. How is wisdom different from knowledge?

2. Where do you need God's wisdom?

3. How do you know you are walking in God's wisdom?

Notes:

WISE MEMORIZE *Action Step:*
Memorize James 1:5 together. Write out the verse on a piece of paper. Say it several times together. Cover one word and read the verse again. Continue to cover a word at a time and read the verse. Cover a word in the middle, end, etc. not just the beginning. In time, you should be able to say the verse without reading it - that's memorization. Now, encourage them to use it daily.

Our Prayer For You:

Jesus, thank you for wisdom. We know the fear of the Lord is the beginning of wisdom (Proverbs 9:10). Help us receive and walk in your wisdom. We desire purity, peace, love, mercy, sincerity, and all the qualities a wise person possesses. Keep us from foolishness and those who do it. In Jesus' name we pray, Amen.

HAVING A BAD DAY

Bible Verse:

"This is the day the Lord has made; We will rejoice and be glad in it."

-Psalm 118:24

Something to Think About:

One bad thing after another can lead to having a bad day. Some days you can feel bad, impatient, irritable, and even sad. You can wake up with a bad attitude and just know it's going to be a rough day. Lack of sleep, depressing news, or busyness can lead to having an negative outlook. Everyone has times in life where they don't feel at their best or desire to interact with others in a loving way. When bad days happen, how do you make it through them? A better question is: how do you change your perspective when bad days occur?

When David wrote Psalm 118, it seems he was having more than a bad day – he was having a few bad years! He began the Psalm with "Give thanks to the Lord", but he is in distress (v. 5), has people who hate him (v. 7), is surrounded by his enemies (vv. 10-12), and threatened by death (v. 17). Instead of allowing these things to overcome him, he rejoices, calls on

Truth to Treasure:
Even on our worst days, God is good.

God for help, trusts, and relies on him for strength, protection, and life. During his bad days, David said, "Give thanks to the Lord, for He is good. His love endures forever" (vv. 1, 29). David knew that day was a day the Lord had made, and he would rejoice it in it (v. 28). The best way to combat a bad day is to praise the Lord!

Bad days will happen. We must remember that God is still in control and always praise Him. The real test of trust is believing in Him during tough times. When life seems like it's unraveling and falling apart, we must praise and trust in God who created everything and holds all things together (Colossians 1:17).

Reflection:

1. What's the best way to overcome a bad mood?

2. How do you respond to a bad day?

3. In what ways are you struggling and how can we pray?

Notes:

THE JESUS JAR *Action Step:*
Grab a jar with a lid. On it, write "Jesus". On a few slips of paper, write bad things that have happened over the last few weeks (or months) in your lives. One by one, read it, pray, write a Scripture on it, and place them in the Jesus Jar. When you begin to feel anxious, mad, etc. about those things, go back to the jar, pull it out, read the Scripture, and pray again before giving it back to Jesus.

Our Prayer For You:

Jesus, thank you for allowing us to be alive this very day. Although it may have some troubles in it, you created it, and we choose to rejoice in it. Thank you for helping us in tough times. You are our help, strength, defender, provider, and source of life. We give thanks because you are good. In Jesus' name we pray, Amen.

MONEY

Bible Verse:

"For where your treasure is, there your heart will be also."

- Matthew 6:21

Something to Think About:

Money is a resource that can be used to buy things we need and even want. We must be careful not to misuse it or see it for more than it really is. It can be something we worry about and even worship. The Apostle Paul said the love of money is the root of all evil (1 Timothy 6:10). He says some have craved it, wandered from the faith, and brought many troubles into their lives from loving it. God gives us resources of money, time, talents, and relationships to use to worship Him and love others. We must learn to use money wisely and for God's glory, not our greed.

Jesus said we should not store up treasures on this earth because they can rust away and be stolen. Earthly riches are temporary. He said we must store up treasures in heaven. What we treasure or think is valuable will be where are heart is (Matthew 6:21). That means what we spend our time, money, and resources on will be what our hearts see as most valuable – that's what we worship. Worshipping money and possessions will let us down every time. They are terrible gods!

Truth to Treasure:
We must honor God with all he gives us.

We must honor God with our finances (Proverbs 3:9). That means we must know what God says about money and possessions. He teaches us to be content with what we have (Hebrews 13:5). He also wants us to be generous (2 Corinthians 9:6-7). We must let God teach us to share and manage our money biblically. This shows God only He sustains us and gives us what we need.

Reflection:

1. How can we love money instead of God?

2. How can our possessions become an idol (something we worship)?

3. How are you being generous with what you have?

Notes:

MY GIVING BANK *Action Step:*
Grab a shoebox, divide the inside into 4 sections with cardboard, and cut a slit in the lid above each one. Label each section below the slit "GIVE 10", "SAVE 10", "BLESS 10", and "SPEND 70". Teach your child that as they receive money (birthday, allowance, chores, etc.), 10% goes to church, 10% goes to savings, 10% goes to help others, and 70% can be used to buy things we need/want.

Our Prayer For You:

Jesus, thank you for giving us everything. What do we have that we did not receive from you (1 Corinthians 4:7)? Help us remember to love and worship you, not money or possessions. We will give you the first part of our money. Help us use a portion to help others. Teach us to be content. In Jesus' name we pray, Amen.

PURPOSE

Bible Verse:

"Before I formed you in the womb I knew you. Before you were born I sanctified you. I ordained you a prophet to the nations."

— Jeremiah 1:5

Something to Think About:

God created us on purpose for a purpose. That purpose is to do His purpose. Sometimes, people ask the questions, "Why did God create me? What is my purpose in life?" At some point, everyone wants to know what they are to be and do with their lives. This is bigger than what career you will have - it is God's purpose for your whole life. God told Jeremiah he made him and had a purpose for his life to be a prophet (a person who speaks for God) (1:5). Our purpose comes from God because He created us. When an inventor makes something, he knows what it is to be used for. As Jeremiah spent time with the Lord, He showed him what he was supposed to do (v. 4). We were created to love and serve God. This can be displayed in many ways.

Truth to Treasure:
I must trust God and obey the purpose He has for my life.

When God shows us His purpose for our lives, we must obey God and do them. Jeremiah made an excuse at first: "I cannot speak, I am too young" (v. 6). God told him not to say that but to obey. God will equip us for what he calls us to be and do. This will require faith – stepping out and trusting God in what He has said.

As you step out and do God's purposes, you will discover how He prepares and supplies all you need. God told Jeremiah He would be with him and give him the words to say. God gave Jeremiah answers for his excuses. He promised to help him do what he called him to do. As we grow closer to God, He will tell us how to live out His plan for our lives. He will also supply all we need and be with us every step of the way. Follow Him. Step out in faith. Let Him work through you!

Reflection:

1. What is God's purpose for our lives?

2. What excuses can we give for not living out God's purposes?

3. How do understand more of God's plan for our lives?

Notes:

WHAT PURPOSE? *Action Step:*
Gather several household items such as a fork, toothbrush, lamp, coin, pillow, etc. and put them in a pile. In one sentence, describe the purpose of an item in the pile (i.e. use to clean your teeth) and have your child retrieve the proper item. Have them describe how they are designed for their purpose. Discuss why you wouldn't use them for a wrong purpose (i.e. use lamp for a pillow).

Our Prayer For You:

Jesus, thank you for creating us on purpose for a purpose. We want to do what you created us to do and be all you created us to be. Help us avoid excuses that would keep us from living on purpose for you. Thank you for being with us and providing everything we need to do you will. In Jesus' name we pray, Amen.

FREEDOM

Bible Verse:

"It is for freedom that Christ has set us free. Stand firm, then, and do not let yourselves be burdened again by a yoke of slavery."
- Galatians 5:1

Something To Think About:

Jesus died on the cross to free us from our sins. Sin causes us to be in bondage. That's like being in jail. When Jesus rose from the grave, he defeated the power sin has over our lives. Paul wrote in Galatians 5:1, "It is for freedom that Christ has set us free." Jesus wants us to be free from sin. Although Jesus frees us from sin by saving us, we can be tempted to return to the bondage of sin. How do we live free and avoid being captured by sin?

Paul continued in Galatians 5:1, "Stand firm, then, and do not let yourselves be burdened again by a yoke of slavery." First, we must stand firm in Jesus. We must stand on God's promises of salvation and freedom from sin. We must believe in His truth and trust His Word. We must remain and abide in Him! He says, "Do not let yourselves be burdened." That means we must choose to act, think, and talk as saved people. We must live out our faith by choosing to live for Christ in all ways. We must not return to the prison chains of sin. Paul said the burden is like a "yoke of slavery". A yoke is a wooden harness that fits over the neck of an animal that makes them go and do what someone wants them to. Sin is a yoke that we must not allow to control our actions, thoughts, and words.

Truth To Treasure:

Only Jesus can free us from sin.

Jesus frees us from sin. In fact, Scripture says, "Whom the Son (Jesus) sets free is free indeed" (John 8:36). Knowing the truth from God's Word sets us free (John 8:32). We must allow Jesus to set us free and choose to walk in His freedom, not going back to being slaves of sin.

Reflection:

1. How is living in sin bondage or like being in jail?

2. Are there any sins in your mind, actions, or words that are keeping you from God's freedom?

3. How do we stay free from sin?

Notes:

Action Step:

FREEDOM COAT

Have your child put on a jacket. Loosely, tie their hands with a string or rope and ask them to take off the jacket. The string/rope restricts them from being free from the jacket. Take a pair of scissors and cut the string/rope. Help them take off the jacket. Discuss how Jesus frees us from sin (string/rope) and sets us free. We cannot get free on our own.

Our Prayer For You:

Jesus, thank you for setting us free. We know when you set us free, we are really free. We want to know more of your truth so we can live freer from sin in our lives. We choose not to give into temptation of sin. We will stand firm in your Word. We will not go back to the sins you have freed us from. In Jesus' name we pray, Amen.

WHERE'S GOD?

Bible Verse:

"You will seek me and find me when you seek me with all your heart."

-Jeremiah 29:13

Something to Think About:

In difficult times, we can be tempted to say, "God, where are you?" It can seem he is a million miles away. This can happen when we wonder why God seems to be allowing something bad to happen and why he doesn't seem to be doing anything to make it better. Acts 17:27 reminds us God is not far from any of us. Jeremiah 29:13 tells us God's promise to his people through his prophet Jeremiah, "You will seek me and find me when you seek me with all your heart." God is not missing when difficulties happen. He is not uncaring or unaware. Jeremiah reminds God's people that although they are facing tough times, he will be with them if they search for him. That's God's promise to us as well.

Truth to Treasure:

In our darkest times, God is near.

When we ask, "God, where are you?" we are really saying, "God, we need you." It's ok to call out to God in prayer when we need him. Many people in the Bible cried out to God for help. David reminds us that God is with us. He said, "You hem me in behind and before and you lay your hand upon me" (Psalm 139:5). He continues by asking more questions than "God, where are you?". He ask, "Where can I go from your Spirit? Where can I flee from your Spirit?" (v. 7). He answers by telling us, "If I go up to the heavens, you are there; if I make my bed in the depths, you are there" (v. 8). When it seems dark, David reminds us, "The darkness is not dark to you...the night will shine like the day, for darkness is as light to you" (vv. 11-12). This means God is present in our darkest moments. When God seems far away, call on Him. He will be found when we seek Him.

Reflection:

1. Why does God seem far away when we face difficulties?

2. How do we know God is with us?

3. Is it ok to ask God to be near and give help?

Notes:

HIDE AND SEEK *Action Step:*
This is an old-fashioned game of Hide and Seek. Take turns hiding from one another. As you find one another, discuss why God seems hard to find at times. If your child has difficulty finding you, give them a hint. Talk about how God helps us find him when we need him. Ask for help when searching for your child and relate that to praying for God to reveal himself when we need him.

Our Prayer For You:

Jesus, thank you for always being present. Sometimes life may seem dark, but you are light. You help us and are near when we need you. Help us keep our eyes on you and not on our problems. Helps us remember you're only a prayer away. Remind us how your Spirit lives in us. In Jesus' name we pray, Amen.

TAKING A STAND

Bible Verse:

"Therefore, put on the full armor of God, so that when the day of evil comes, you may be able to stand your ground, and after you have done everything, to stand."

-Ephesians 6:13

Something to Think About:

There are many things out of our control in this life. None of us can make someone else do the right thing. However, when someone is doing the wrong thing, we can choose where we will stand – with them or with God. There will be times when you will have to "take a stand" for what is right. Always side with God's Word boldly, yet humbly. Never stand for what is sinful (Psalm 1:1). Some people will stand for the right things but do it in a wrong way. They can be mean, rude, and foolish. God wants us to always display all the fruit of the Spirit in our lives. Love, joy, peace, patience, kindness, goodness, faithfulness, gentleness, and self-control are required as we stand for righteousness and truth.

The best way to take a stand is to put on the Armor of God (Ephesians 6:13-18). The Apostle Paul tells us, "When the day of evil comes, stand your ground." We do this in prayer as we humbly on the Word of God, with righteousness and truth, in faith as the people of God saved by the Gospel.

Truth to Treasure:
Always stand with God in all things and at all times.

When should you "take a stand"? Isaiah 1:17 says, "Learn to do right; seek justice. Defend the oppressed. Take up the cause of the fatherless; plead the case of the widow." These are great times to "take a stand" by serving others. Taking a stand has little to do with announcing what you are against and more to do with living what God is for. Choose to always stand on God's side in all things and at all times. This means be a doer of the Word (James 1:22-26), avoid evil (1 Thessalonians 5:22), and love the least of these (Matthew 25:34-40).

Reflection:

1. How do we "take a stand" for God?

2. How can we stand for truth in the wrong way?

3. In what way should you take a stand for God and His truth now?

Notes:

Action Step:
STAND ON THE WORD
Read Matthew 25:34-40. One way to take a stand is by serving those Jesus called "the least of these". Make a list of the types of people Jesus mentions in this Scripture. Under each, write how you can serve a couple of these in the next week or so. Discuss how one way of standing on the side of truth is living out God's Word in obedience by loving others.

Our Prayer For You:

Jesus, thank you for showing us through your Word the truth with which we should always stand. Help us exhibit your fruit of the Spirit as we stand for truth. Convict us by your Spirit when we stand in sin. Teach us to live out your truth by loving others and pointing them to Jesus. In Jesus' name we pray, Amen.

DON'T GIVE UP

Bible Verse:

"Let us not become weary in doing good, for at the proper time we will reap a harvest if we do not give up. Therefore, as we have opportunity, let us do good to all people."   -Galatians 6:9-10

Something to Think About:

Obeying God's Word and doing good are very rewarding. There will be times when you get tired as you do them. When you are tired, you will feel like giving up and stopping. Whatever you do, don't give up following Jesus! That was the encouragement the Apostle Paul gave the followers of Jesus in several churches in region of Galatia after warning them of several things to avoid (Galatians 5:1-6:8). He told them not to give up doing good because "at the proper time we will reap a harvest" (Galatians 6:9). Paul knew they would feel overwhelmed by all of his instructions and the responsibilities in following Jesus. They needed encouragement, a so do we, as we walk in step with the Spirit and obey God's Word.

Truth to Treasure:

Don't give up as you follow God.

We will be rewarded by Jesus when we follow Jesus. Paul says we will "reap a harvest". What is this? The reward of eternity with Jesus is for all who are saved from their sins. We can't earn this – it is a gift from Jesus as we repent of our sins (John 3:16; Romans 6:23). Paul said, "I have fought the good fight, I have finished the race, I have kept the faith. Now there is in store for me the crown of righteousness, which the Lord, the righteous Judge, will award to me on that day–and not only to me, but also to all who have longed for his appearing." The reward of following Jesus in this life is eternity in the next with Him! Reaping a harvest can also be seeing others come to salvation as we share the gospel with them. Don't give up on telling other how to be saved by Jesus. Ultimately, the best thing we get from following Jesus wholeheartedly is the ability to worship him. To God be the glory! Great things He has done!

Reflection:

1. Why is encouragement needed as we follow Jesus?

2. When it comes to following Jesus, what causes us to become weary and consider giving up?

3. What are the rewards for following Jesus?

Notes:

A GOOD REWARD *Action Step:*
In one or more ice cube trays, place a quarter in each space. Fill with water and freeze. Say: "If we want a good reward, we must not give up." Place all the ice cubes (14+) in a large clear container. Tell your child they can have the money if they will wait for them to melt. Pray about how to use the money. Talk about the lesson each time you check on the ice and quarters.

Our Prayer For You:

Jesus, thank you for the honor of following you. Help us not give up when we get tired as we follow you. Refresh our hearts and minds as we serve you. Keep our us focused on the benefits of growing in Christ and seeing others come to the faith. Thank you for the eternal reward of heaven. In Jesus' name we pray, Amen.

"Hear, O Israel: The Lord our God, the Lord is one. Love the Lord your God with all your heart and with all your soul and with all your strength. These commandments that I give you today are to be on your hearts. Impress them on your children. Talk about them when you sit at home and when you walk along the road, when you lie down and when you get up. Tie them as symbols on your hands and bind them on your foreheads. Write them on the doorframes of your houses and on your gates."

-Deuteronomy 6:4-9

OTHER BOOKS BY STEPHEN HARRISON

The Biblical Elder: A Twelve-Week Journey in Biblical Eldership (2021)

One-on-One Discipleship: 52 Discipleship Lessons Designed to Help Disciples Make Disciples of Jesus (2021)

25 Jesus-Filled Days of Christmas: Devotionals to Help Families Keep Their Eyes on Jesus (2022)

My Refuge and Strength: A 150-Day Journey Through Psalms (2022)

How to Have Inner Joy While Experiencing Utter Chaos: 10 Weeks of Increasing Joy in Jesus -A Daily Devotional Study in Philippians (2023)

The Biblical Deacon: A Twelve-Week Journey in Biblical Servanthood (2023)

The Proverbs Man: 31 Days of Walking in God's Wisdom (2024)

Find these on Amazon.com

Visit www.stephenrharrison.com for more of Stephen's writing and to order books.

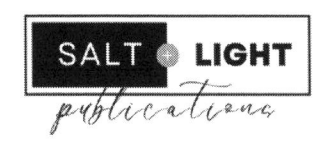

Made in the USA
Columbia, SC
25 September 2024